At the Lord's Table

At the Lord's Table

Ralph G. Turnbull

BAKER BOOK HOUSE
Grand Rapids, Michigan

PHOTOLITHOPRINTED BY CUSHING - MALLOY, INC.
ANN ARBOR, MICHIGAN, UNITED STATES OF AMERICA

Introduction . . . .

"What mean ye by this service?" (Exodus 12:26) is a question often asked and answered. From the Passover to the Lord's Supper the story is retold in the light of what took place at the first Passover. For the Jews in Egypt and then the Messiah in Jerusalem both Passover and Lord's Supper are set within the framework of a record handed down from one generation to another.

Believing that Jesus promised to build the church with people out of all nations and cultures, He gave them this central rite to be carried out regularly as a reminder of His teaching and especially of His death and sacrifice. Paul claimed that he had "received of the Lord" (I Corinthians 11:23) that which was handed on to others. Thus a tradition was established based upon history and experience, revelation and Scripture.

In the interpretation of the words dealing with the Lord's Supper certain premises are assumed. One is that this Last Supper issued from the Passover feast. The critical discussion of the Gospel records has been considered and the evidence weighed in favor of this point of view. As the church succeeds Israel as the people of God, so the Lord's Supper is the fulfilment of the Passover. Another is that the presence of Christ is a spiritual, personal relationship which is symbolized by the use of material elements and spoken of by words of Jesus having transcendent meaning.

These meditations are suggestive in preparation for the reception of the Lord's Supper. The Bible has many passages and texts which point to the sufferings and death of Christ. Here we have limited the selection to those references in the New Testament which are used directly in connection with the actual celebration. Of the five basic passages, there are three records of the institution in the Gospels of Matthew,

Mark, and Luke, and two by Paul in I Corinthians 10 and 11. Included also is the teaching of John 6.

Two books have preceded this in an endeavor to share a personal faith and to minister as a pastor to congregations who have been part of the rich heritage of that same faith. *The Seven Words from the Cross* (1956) and *The Pathway to the Cross* (1959) constitute the background out of which has come this fresh attempt to discover more light and truth related to the central mystery of our redemption.

Christians of all communions will have other insights as we enter the holy of holies, but God's people who gather at the Lord's Table are "all one in Christ Jesus." In that light and spirit it is hoped that the reader will benefit by a reverent approach to this sacred and joyous experience at the Lord's Table.

RALPH G. TURNBULL

The First Presbyterian Church
of Seattle, Washington

Contents . . . .

I. A Partnership

Two are better than one; because they have a good reward for their labor. For if they fall, the one will lift up his fellows but woe to him that is alone when he falleth; for he hath not another to help him up. And if one prevail against him, two shall withstand him; and a threefold cord is not quickly broken."

— Ecclesiastes 4:12

Ye have not chosen me, but I have chosen you.

— John 15:16

I. A Partnership

"Partakers of the Lord's Table."

— I Corinthians 10:21

The table is the symbol of fellowship and family. There we gather in our common life and share together the common meal of the home. Christianity began in a home when Jesus called two disciples to follow him. They abode with him that day and in that home the beginning of the church is recorded (John 1:35-39). The Gospels tell of similar gatherings in homes. Jesus was welcomed especially at Bethany. What an interior that was! The friends of Jesus gave him hospitality and they shared together in the meal at the table. In the last talk of Jesus in the Upper Room he spoke of how God loved his disciples and how "we will come unto him, and make our abode with him" (John 14:23). The Christian experience here is that of the life of God in the soul of man — coming to dwell as in a home. In the letter to Laodicea our Lord stands at the door and knocks. If one hears and opens the door he said, "I will come in to him, and will sup with him, and he with me" (Rev. 3:20). Here again is the language of the home and the table at the center.

One of the chief functions of the Lord's Supper is to manifest the partnership of Jesus with his own. There is a sharing and fellowship found here far more profound than any other.

1. *It Is the Lord's Table*

This is the distinctive mark of the meeting place of our Lord and his disciples. We have our own homes and in them the common meeting place around our table. There the family gathers each day and shares in conversation and eating. The address on the street and the particular building of our home tells of one family dwelling there. Our family table has memories and associations which are sacred over the years. As children leave home and go out into the world on their own, they carry with them the tender ties of family life around the table.

Other associations in life bring to mind the use of the table as a meeting place and an occasion of sharing one with another. The many clubs, fraternities, organizations, and societies afford opportunity to meet with others of like mind. There is the interchange of idea and speech; there is the mutual recognition of others in a common bond which allows us to work together for good ends. The most common and most popular meeting place is at a meal. There at some table men and women gather to become partners in noble causes. But not everyone is invited and not anyone can share. There are tests of character, position, and ability before one is admitted to partnership at the table.

In contrast, this is the Lord's Table. As in the Upper Room in that home in Jerusalem, our Lord invited several men to join him. They were not selected for any special goodness in themselves but chosen only by his sovereign love for a service to be rendered thereafter. What a mixed group they were! Within them were the seeds of disloyalty, treachery, false ambition, jealousy, and defection. Nevertheless, this was the Lord's Table then — and now. Here in our day we gather at his invitation. We come from every walk in life and in various degrees of faith and commitment. He has called us and we have responded. The Table is not labeled as Presbyterian or any other religious name. This is the *Lord's* Table and he bids us welcome.

2. *It Is a Distinctive Table*

One reason why this table is marked off from all others lies in its historic significance. At the first the Christians gathered around in their homes and meeting places in the knowledge that they had broken with their dead past. For those in Corinth at least, they had come out of idolatrous worship in a heathen temple. In that temple was the darkness of evil and the pollution of immorality. Paul urged them to "flee idolatry" (v. 14). They could not afford to look back or play with the old life. In that clear-cut decision they now came to the Lord's Table in contrast to the "table of demons" (v. 21). The latter was associated with indulgence and debauchery. The Lord's Table is associated with committal to the new and pure life.

That table reaches back over the centuries to the Upper Room. It has lasted over nineteen hundred years. With the circle of the years it has endured many other tests and survived many attacks against its existence.

> Saints of the early dawn of Christ,
>   Saints of Imperial Rome,
> Saints of the cloistered Middle Age,
>   Saints of the modern home;
> Saints of the soft and sunny East,
>   Saints of the frozen seas,
> Saints of the isles that wave their palms
>   In the far Antipodes;
> Saints of the marts and busy streets,
>   Saints of the squalid lanes,
> Saints of the silent solitudes,
>   Of the prairies and the plains;
> Saints who were wafted to the skies
>   In the torment robe of flame,
> Saints who have graven on men's thoughts
>   A monumental name . . .

O God-lit cloud of witness
Souls of the sainted dead.

— J. Marchant
Deeds Done for Christ

From the catacombs of Rome; from the Huguenots of France;
from the Covenanters of Scotland; from the martyrs of
Europe; from the Puritans and Pilgrims to the New World
— they have met at the Lord's Table as one in Christ.

3. *It Is a Family Table*

As in our home the family gathers around, so at the
Lord's Table is the meeting of *the Family of God*. Nowhere
else is this demonstrated or carried out so well. Here we
are united in faith and spirit. Sharing as partners with our
Lord, we share with each other and witness to our partnership and fellowship. Christians with different cultures, of
various color, having other names and labels are drawn
together as one in Christ. The labels of men disappear and
we think only of our Lord whom we worship.

There is but *one table*. Myriads are in use all over the
world, but still there is only one table. There is also "one
body." "We being many are one bread, and one body: for
we are all partakers of that one bread" (v. 17). Whatever
differences of attitude or points of view concerning life, the
Table of the Lord unites us. To be a partaker has only one
basis: "by grace — a partaker" (v. 30). At the Lord's Table
we testify to the fact that God's grace has reached us and
made us partakers of his life and love. In this truth the
family of God unites: "whether, therefore, ye eat, or drink,
or whatsoever ye do, do all to the glory of God" (v. 31).

Background:
"Now ye are the body of Christ, and members in particular" — I Corinthians 12:27
"Ye are a chosen generation, a royal priesthood, an holy
nation, a peculiar people . . . which in time past were
not a people, but are now the people of God. . . ."
— I Peter 2:9,10

II. A Memorial

According to thy gracious Word,
  In meek humility,
This will I do, my dying Lord,
  I will remember thee.

Thy body, broken for my sake,
  My bread from heaven shall be;
Thy testamental cup I take
  And thus remember thee.

Remember thee and all thy pains,
  And all thy love to me!
Yea, while a breath, a pulse remains,
  Will I remember thee.

And, when these failing lips grow dumb,
  And mind and memory flee,
When thou shalt in thy kingdom come,
  Jesus, remember me.

— James Montgomery

II. A Memorial

"This do in remembrance of me."

— I Corinthians 11:24

The institution of the Lord's Supper takes us back to the Upper Room where Jesus gathered with his twelve apostles. It was the time of Passover and devout Jews celebrated this feast annually. That night Jesus was betrayed by Judas and was led to trial and death. Surrounding this event are many truths, but uppermost is that of remembrance. It was our Lord's teaching that what he said and did should not be forgotten.

1. *The Memorial Is Rooted in History*

When the Passover was carried through as an ordinance of God for the Hebrew people, Jesus shared in this. He had attended many in his lifetime, but now for the last time he acts as the Host and Leader of the feast. The Gospels and the Book of Exodus (cf. Background references) give the details. We read and reread them a thousand times and still they speak to us of that "last, dark hour." Christians everywhere do not need to be convinced that here is the greatest drama ever staged. On the eve of the cross with its crucifixion and death, was the hour of our Lord's preparation. He anticipated his death and told his followers about it. He prepared himself for that experience not only by prayer in the Garden of Gethsemane but in this service in the Upper Room. There he talked to his own (cf. John 13-17) and there he gave them this to remember.

Our Lord worked miracles, but he did not specifically ask to be remembered by demonstrations of his power. He talked in memorable parables and sayings, but he did not ask to be remembered by his words alone, marvellous though they are. He asked to be remembered by this one supreme act of laying down his life in death, even the death of the cross. Jesus instituted a church to be built to endure throughout the ages, yet he did not ask to be remembered by an institution. Here in the Lord's Supper we are taken back to that Upper Room where he gave this ordinance as a means of memorial. Rooted in history is the story of how twelve men met with the Master and received from him the Hebrew Passover which was then merged into the Communion of the Lord's Supper. The Old Covenant was superseded by the New Covenant. What we 'remember' is rooted in history.

2. *The Memorial Is Related to Experience*

Here and now we recall the events and deeds. Jesus is not some dim, shadowy figure of the past: He is alive and with us now. Memory is not the same for everyone. Some there are who have good and acute memories: others have poor memories and forget easily. A slate is wiped clean by a sponge and how near this seems to some who would like to recall the past. Memory can be trained and improved and there is nothing embarassing in that. Our weekly Sunday services enable us to remember God, to honor and worship Him. Our birthdays open the way for acts of love and kindness. National holidays recall historic hours which still speak to us. The Lord's Supper is another of God's ways to help us "remember."

In the intepretation of this Supper we see that this is a memorial act in which all Christians share and not the

Mass in which only a priest functions. This is not the repetition of a sacrifice, but the commemoration of a sacrifice made "once for all" (Heb. 9:28), never to be repeated. After World War I and World War II many monuments were erected in cities and towns across the English-speaking world. Names were inscribed in Books of Remembrance so that people might not forget the service and sacrifice of those who fought for freedom. Visit some of those monuments today, and sadly we report that many are neglected and forgotten. Even at the annual occasion of memorial with a service or celebration, only a minority attend. An Armistice Day or Memorial Day are no longer occasions when the multitude stops its feverish life or when voices are hushed and sounds muted for a little. Men forget. The Lord's Supper enables us to remember Jesus.

3. *The Memorial Is Regulated to Faith*

According to our faith we share and receive. Not everyone has the same measure of faith, but all may share in this celebration. The young as well as the old may partake. There is a wise adjustment to the individual who comes to the Table. Memorials vary and appreciation is different. Visit Lincoln's Memorial in Washington, D.C. Climb the steps to the heights and stand looking in on that majestic carved figure seated there. Read the surrounding extracts from his famous speeches and feel the thrill of being there with history. In a moment memory brings to us the struggle of a nation, the new birth of freedom, the tragic death of Abraham Lincoln — and we are awed and silent. There is a hush over us and those who stand by. Strangers from afar may not feel this as those who are loyal citizens of America. Adjustment of appreciation comes because of what we know and believe.

Thus it is with the Lord's Supper. This memorial is not in wood or stone or sculptured by the skill of man. This is a *living* memorial. At the resting place of David Livingstone, the missionary, in Westminster Abbey, London, is a tablet of testimony to his character and deeds. It was *Punch,* that joyful magazine, which paid him a rich tribute

by staying: "David Livingstone — here is 'living stone!'" At
the Table of our Lord — here is a *living* memorial. It is not
dead or cold: it is alive and warm. It is universal in its sweep
and perpetual in its use. It is simple, yet sublime. Wherever
observed it is glorious, because we are face to face with Jesus.
At the Table of the Lord we find faith and trust are sufficient
to enable us to take from him all that we need. We come as
those who remember him.

What is this act of remembrance? Is it not the means of
confessing our faith in Christ as our Saviour? Do we not
express our love and devotion to him who now holds us in
thrall as his slaves? There are those who have wandered from
home and family and all that is fairest and best and tried
to blot out the past in their sin. But let a scrap of paper
name a certain town; let an old song come over the radio;
let a sprig of heather or a flower be seen — and at once the
imagination can see again the old ways and people and
places. Men do not forget forever. The heart cannot banish
that haunting music and stifle those dreams recalling other
and better days. Thus it is with us who come to the Table of
the Lord. Here is no tomb but a table! As we gather around
we engage in the finest hour of remembrance. We recall again
our Lord's love for us; his sacrifice on the cross; his victory
over sin and death; and our oneness with him who are now
his.

"Remember me," said the Saviour.
"I will remember thee," answers his disciple.

Background:
"This do in remembrance of me." — Luke 22:19
"In remembrance of me...." — I Corinthians 11:25
"This day shall be unto you for a memorial; and ye shall
keep it a feast to the Lord throughout your generations;
ye shall keep it a feast by an ordinance for ever."
                                                                    — Exodus 12:14

III. A Witness

Come, to the Supper come,
Sinners, there still is room;
Every soul may be his guest,
Jesus gives the general word;
Share the monumental feast,
Eat the supper of the Lord.

In this authentic sign
Behold the stamp divine:
Christ revives his sufferings here,
Still exposes them to view;
See the Crucified appear,
Now believe he died for you.
— Charles Wesley

III. A Witness

"Ye do show the Lord's death."

— I Corinthians 11:26

At the heart of the Lord's Supper is the fact that God's people set forth the glory of the ~~evangel or~~ good news of the Saviour. What was a farewell meal on the part of our Lord was at the same time an anticipation of the Messianic banquet to come. With that kingdom in view this enactment took place to keep alive the memory of Christ's sacrifice on the cross. Between the death of the cross and the coming kingdom victory is this particular deed. Here is a witness to the Christian faith.

1. *Every Christian Is a Witness*

The evangelical nature of the Last Supper is unfolded by the acts of individual Christians who unite in a common meal. At the beginning the early Christians met in their homes for their regular meal. At the close of that meal they would take bread and wine and commemorate the death of their Lord. Paul found at Corinth that some people over ate and over drank, so that when they came to partake of the memorial meal they were unfit to do so. Thus he counselled separating the two. In this way a more definite meaning was given to the Last Supper celebration. Every Christian partaking was on his honor and faced with the necessity of knowing the sacredness of that act. The act became a preachment.

The church over the centuries has gradually given to the pastor the privilege of being the preacher to a congregation even as the evangelist has ministered to those without. In so doing something has been lost by the people. More and more they have left preaching or witnessing to a select few and neglected something which is for all. This does not minimize the fact that God still calls individuals to preach as a full time vocation. The fact is that at the beginning every Christian was expected to be a witness. Acts 1:8 directs, "Ye shall receive power, the Holy Spirit coming upon you; and ye shall be witnesses unto me, both in Jerusalem, and in Samaria, and in Judaea, and unto the uttermost parts of the earth." If this is to be carried out, how can Christians do this alongside of the men set apart to preach? By their lives, their conduct, and their words of witness, they have done this. And yet there is still this significant way — at the Lord's Table. Here every one partaking is a witness and a preacher. Here each one confesses that Christ is his Saviour and that the sacrifice of the cross is the one obligation for the sins of the world. In that act of sharing there is preaching and witnessing.

2. *Christ's Death Is Central*

The glory of the Christian faith has ever been in this foundational truth. The evangel or gospel is not pointing to the life of a good man or to the sublime teaching of the greatest teacher or to a code of rules by which ethical standards are raised up. These have value but they do not in themselves constitute the evangel. The evangel centers in the death of the cross. At its heart God suffered and in Christ took upon himself the sin of the world. Those who witness are forgiven people. They are not puffed up with pride in their own self-satisfaction. They are now humbled at the knowledge how God loved them and gave himself for them.

The broken body and the shed blood (I Cor. 11:24, 25) are stressed in unmistakable terms so that we could not be misled about what we do in witnessing. The Negro Spiritual asks: "Were you there when they crucified my Lord " Yes, in the Lord's Supper every believing heart can confess that we were there. We have stood by the cross and we have seen the spectacle and we have heard the words from the Crucified. That is why our hymns take up the strain of this death of deaths. "When I survey the wondrous cross. . . ." "Nothing in my hands I bring, Simply to Thy cross I cling. . . ." "Jesus paid it all, All to Him I owe. . . ." Whether in the majestic hymns of the church or the more recent gospel hymns of folk-song type — the one refrain runs. Or go through the New Testament and read the messages, sermon reports, or the plain teaching, and one thing is clear — the emphasis on the death of Jesus Christ on the cross — the *kerygma* — the redeeming gospel message. Our salvation depends upon that death.

3. *The Gospel Is Proclaimed*

Here is a declaration which has no rival. Across the ages the proclamation of this truth has changed multitudes. Paul cries, "ye do show the Lord's death," and in that verb he gives the emphasis for every witness. When we share in the Lord's Supper we are preaching or proclaiming the gospel. The verb (*katangello*) does not suggest a showing forth in the sense of repeating that death, but rather a proclamation of it. Here is preaching in an action sermon. The witnesses take the elements of bread and wine and using them as signs and seals of Christ's death we proclaim in deed and word the nature of the gospel. The question might be asked — where is the congregation for this proclamation? Always around an occasion like this are those who are looking on — the young with their eager questions, ever learning the Christian faith; the casual and the indifferent to be reminded of their need of Christ; the unseen host of angels (for did not Peter declare that "these are things the angels long to see into" — (I Peter 1:8-12). And do we not reconfirm to ourselves that it is in this gospel we have been made Christ's men and women?

The Table becomes a pulpit. The bread and wine become the acted Word. The witnesses become evangelists. At the Supper we proclaim a feast and not a fast. The gospel is good news of sins forgiven and heaven assured. In announcing this we are highly honored as God's servants. No, he calls us no longer "servants" but *friends* (John 15:14). Towards God we affirm our faith; towards ourselves we reaffirm that we believe; and towards men we announce the saving word. The sharing in this experience at the Lord's Supper is not a means of salvation: we are here because we are His already. Nevertheless, God can use this to open blinded eyes. At a service in Edinburgh, "Rabbi" Duncan, Professor and humble Christian, was passing the elements when a dear woman shrank back as if to say she was unworthy even to partake of that rich fare. At which the kindly heart of Duncan said to her: "Woman, tak' it; it's for sinners like us!" Yes, only the sinful can be forgiven and only the forgiven take from the pierced hand of the Master.

At the Lord's Table we witness to the gospel for by this word is the word of the gospel preached.

> We may not know, we cannot tell;
> What pains He had to bear;
> But we believe it was for us,
> He hung and suffered there.

Background:

The New Testament uses several words for the proclamation of the gospel. The word *katangello* means to declare and is translated "to show" in I Corinthians 11:26. Here the verb indicates that the partaking of the elements at the Lord's Supper is a proclamation of an evangel of the Lord's death.

IV. A Forecast

Till He come": Oh, let the words
Linger on the trembling cords:
Let the little while between
In their golden light be seen;
Let us think how heaven and home
Lie beyond that — "Till He come.
— E. H. Bickersteth

In the fading of the starlight
We can see the coming morn;
And the lights of men are paling
In the splendours of the dawn;
For the eastern skies are glowing
As with lights of hidden fire,
And the hearts of men are stirring
With the throb of deep desire.

IV. A Forecast

"Till He come." — I Corinthians 11:26

Our Lord's departure would leave the apostles as orphans. This disturbed his followers. What of the future if left alone? Here our Lord promised that he would return. This does not refer to the promised coming of the Holy Spirit (cf. John 14). The Second Advent was not the baptism of the Holy Spirit at Pentecost or any other affusion of the Spirit. Some three hundred times in the New Testament the subject of the Second Advent is mentioned as an eminent doctrine. It is linked with the final victory of the coming Kingdom of God.

In the Gospels our Lord is on record as telling about his second advent. Particular words are used which bear but one meaning — an act of coming and a presence or arrival. Our Lord's views about the Last Things cannot be set aside as unimportant in the light of his teaching. Paul relates this truth to the Lord's Supper where we anticipate Christ's return and the victory of the Kingdom of God.

1. *It Strengthens Our Faith*

At the Table the Christian *looks back*. We recall what our Lord has done for us. There at the Cross he died for our sins and gave us forgiveness and eternal life. Now we meet to remember this in a unique fellowship of faith. Personal

31

faith is linked with community faith; the one with the
many. That faith in Christ as our Saviour is not alone the
death of deaths: it also brings something to life now and it
sees clearly what is in the future. That death of the cross
was the beach-head or D-Day as the battle began on the
enemy's territory. In the mind of Christ so engaged there was
the anticipation of V-Day yet to come when the enemy would
be finally and completely overcome. This is the faith of the
church and has been throughout the ages.

In Matthew 16:13-17 our Lord speaks of the building of
the *church;* then of the sacrifice of the *cross;* and finally of
his *coming.* There can be no doubt that his prediction about
the church is steadily being realized in the universal and
worldwide church. The death of the cross was preceded by
his sufferings given in some detail and this was carried out.
It is inconceivable that he would fail to fulfill his pledge
and prophecy concerning his promised coming again. In the
same language used about the church and the cross He speaks
of the coming. The *fact* is declared; the fashion is indicated;
and the climax is described. This is part of the Christian
faith.

2. *It Satisfies Our Love*

Faith looks back to the accomplished deed of saving us at
awful cost. Now at the Table we *look up* in devotion and
loyalty as we express our love to Christ. The Second Advent
forecast is a means of satisfaction. What is the end and goal
of our struggle and temptation as we live the Christian life?
Many Christians find this perplexing and mysterious when
they pass through trials and difficulties. Here at the Table
we are enabled to take our bearings and chart our course.
The baffling providences of life are seen in a new light. With
the promise that Christ will return in victory and in glory
we now partake of the elements of *His* love for us and at
the same time express *our* love to Him. There is a satisfaction
generated within us.

Love is the greatest thing in the world. Yes! when it is

divine love and not the sentimental idea of the novelist. That holy love has reached us and now we are remade by it so that the stirring of it within wells up and out to God through Christ. We love him because he first loved us. Such love is now expressed in deeds to others, but it is manifested in this action at the Table where love centers again in Christ. Between the cross and the coming is set the communion. Here we tell (as it were) our Lord that we love him and that we are waiting for his coming again. This is the hour of banquet and of song: it is also the time of expressing love.

3. *It Stimulates Our Hope*

The second advent is the hope of the Christian and of the church. At the Table we also *look on*. Prophecy has both the idea of preaching to the present and prediction about the future. The prophets so proclaimed. Our Lord also spoke in this way, and Paul so interprets. The latter meaning is in view here. In this action of love we find hope alive. This hope is the personal return of our Saviour. Time or circumstances are not important here, but only the fact that the Belovèd One (Eph. 1:6) is coming! We are doing this while we wait for him. We long for his presence in that deeper sense.

When the followers of Prince Charles, known as Jacobites, waited for and looked for their Prince to come from over the water in France during the seventeenth century, they waited with expectancy. Then in their longing for his appearing they expressed that in a strong hope. In every cup of wine they drank they pledge their loyalty; in every song sung they renewed their oath to serve him. It was this hope which kept alive their strength to fight his battles. The hope of the Christian is stimulated when we are at the table.

Every one that has this hope in him purifies himself even as he is pure. The kingdom is coming when the King returns. This hope stimulates to a devout life, a devotion to service, and it sustains in death in seeing the beyond.

The parabolic teaching undoubtedly stresses this theme.

Parables tell of a period of absence on the part of Christ; his leaving and then his return. Christ is the center of these messages — as the One going and returning. The plain teaching also includes references to a coming again and of a climax to history in terms of harvest, the end of the age, and the last day. While the actual day is shrouded in the secrets of God, there are signs to be observed as portents of that coming day.

There is an inherent fitness and a moral necessity for the Second Advent. Man's failure to govern himself adequately and justly; the moral collapse of society; and the demonic tides of evil sweeping the world — these are indications of a need to be met only by the King of kings coming to reign in righteousness. World conditions do not point to any human solution to world problems. God who came in Christ at the First Advent must surely come again in the Second Advent. It is this which is celebrated in part at the Lord's Table. The forecast brings foregleams of that day and hour when we shall see him face to face.

Background:

    "In my Father's kingdom. . . ." — Matthew 26:29

V. A Covenant

My broken body thus I give
For you, for all; take, eat, and live;
And oft the sacred rite renew
That brings my wondrous love to view.

My blood I thus pour forth, he cries,
To cleanse the soul in sin that lies;
In this the covenant is sealed,
And heaven's eternal grace revealed.
— John Morrison

V. A Covenant

"This cup is the new testament."
— I Corinthians 11:25

Many times in the New Testament we are reminded of this truth — that we are not our own; we have been bought with a price. In this God has entered our lives and bound us to himself. A covenant in our modern way of thinking speaks of two people entering into an agreement one with another. Each obligates himself to the other for the purchase and sale of a house or a solemn arrangement to act together as when nations pledge to stand together in a crisis. A paper is usually signed and sealed with the necessary safeguards of law and order and witnessed as authentic in deed and intent. The Hebrew meaning differs somewhat in that One Person has bound himself with an oath to act on our behalf in the sense of "promise." In this light we see the truth.

1. *Sign and Seal of Grace*

The marks of this pledge by God in Christ are found in the Lord's Supper itself whereby we see how he alone instituted this. Therein is the setting apart of things seen and handled as visible symbols of the unseen and eternal. That God should choose to select material objects for this act is not a surprise. In the birth and life of our Lord Jesus Christ we have the supreme demonstration of this principle. In what is known as the Incarnation God took hold of human nature and the common round of our lowly life. The ordinary things of life became a means of grace and were touched by the divine. Nothing thereafter need be secular or unclean but all of life could be holy and sacred.

In taking bread and wine in the Lord's Supper our Lord uses elements common to man's daily use as signs and seals of his grace. A flag of our country is a sign and seal: it reminds us of our national life and our part in it as citizens. A ring given in marriage is a sign and seal of the confidence and trust two people have in each other as they pledge themselves to be one in God's sight. The use of bread and wine is another unusual sign and seal. Uniquely, these elements are not used alone — there is always the *Word* of God which accompanies them. The seal is not separated from the evidence or else you have only bread and wine. But when the Word of God is spoken and received by faith in using the bread and the wine, then the common use is exchanged for that spiritual use intended. Thus Word and material element together constitute the sign and seal.

2. *Ordinance and Sacrament of Love*

Words change their meaning over the years, hence our need to interpret these words. An ordinance is a religious observance of a certain order, a use ordered by authority. In this Christ has ordained and ordered we act in this way at the Table. The word "sacrament" comes from the Latin use when a soldier took an oath of allegiance to the emperor and bound himself to serve. Whatever else is mysterious, this is clear — in this action at the Table we take an oath of loyalty to Jesus Christ. We also renew our vows of devotion to him.

The early Christians knew what this meant, living as they did in the Roman Empire with its power structure. They knew that in coming to the Table they vowed to live and die if need be for their Lord and Master. They fought in a spiritual warfare, but the action took place in the areas of human relations. In society, business, home, and politics they lived their lives as Christ's men marked off by their commitment to *the* Lord of life. Nero might claim their lives as citizens by his taxes and demands, but Jesus Christ claimed the whole of life for his kingdom.

3. *Pledge and Commitment of Loyalty*

The Table brings us face to face with our Lord. We are reminded anew of the vows we have taken, either in baptism or in public profession of our Christian faith. We are "in the world, but not of the world." We are now the people of God. We belong to two kingdoms — the earthly and the spiritual. The Hebrews used to cut a covenant by cutting their skin and mingling blood with blood as a bond of friendship and faith. As God bound himself to Israel long ago, so now the Old Covenant is superseded by the New Covenant "in His blood." The New is the Second Covenant and the Better Covenant. Thus "the blood of the Covenant" binds us as nothing else. Christ died *for us*.

On February 28, 1638 the Scottish National Covenant was signed on parchment in Greyfriar's Churchyard, Edinburgh, as Christian men and women become · Covenanters. That parchment, in possession of the Edinburgh Town Council today, shows that there are signatures in *blood!* Out of this came the Solemn League and Covenant in 1648 whereby the Reformed Faith was affirmed in Scotland. In the Upper Room our Lord signed and sealed himself to his people. We now return that at the Table of communion when we observe the rite. This is the hour of our commitment anew to show our loyalty to him. We own that in the death of the cross he made us his own. Gladly we stand at the salute and in fealty we pledge our lives in return!

While there are few references to a covenant in the New Testament the idea is always present. God comes to his people and there is a binding back to him in several ways. What God began in Abraham he now completes in Christ (cf. Gal. 4:6-9). The letter to the *Hebrews* indicates how the New Covenant is better than the Old Covenant. The latter idea and use of the covenant came to have a classical thought in terms of testament. Whereas the covenant had a legal institution in ancient times, our Lord used it as something more personal. The Old Testament had its blood-covenant and relation, but now the blood was that of the testator given to the one to benefit by the will.

Here is the disposition of God carried out to all who put their trust in him. His saving purpose is revealed. Judas made a covenant with the authorities of Israel to sell out his Master. He placed upon him the price of a slave in thirty pieces of silver. Our Lord Jesus made a covenant with his own to bind his disciples to him even as he bound himself to us forever. Judas took the symbol of man's pride and success — money. Jesus gave in the symbol of God's grace and self-sacrifice — blood! Superior to the Old Covenant is that of the New Covenant. In Christ the covenant is the "new," the "second," and the "better" (cf. Heb. 9:15; 7:22; 8:7).

> I hear the words of love,
> I gaze upon the blood,
> I see the mighty Sacrifice,
> And I have peace with God.
> — Horatius Bonar

Background:

"This is the blood of the new testament."
— Matthew 26:28

"This is my blood of the new testament." — Mark 14:24

"This cup is the new testament in my blood."
— Luke 22:20

"For this cause he is the mediator of the new testament."
— Hebrews 9:15

VI. A Communion

We taste thee, O thou living Bread,
  And long to feast upon thee still;
We drink of thee, the Fountain-head,
  And thirst our souls from thee to fill.

Our restless spirits yearn for thee,
  Where'er our changeful lot is cast;
Glad, when thy gracious smile we see,
  Blest, when our faith can hold thee fast.
                                        — Bernard of Clairvaux

VI. A Communion

> *"The cup of blessing which we bless, is it not
> the communion of the blood of Christ? The
> bread which we break, is it not the commun-
> ion of the body of Christ?"*
>
> — I Corinthians 10:16

The Lord's Supper is generally known as the *Communion*
and the Table as the *Communion Table*. Thus we have been
given the true and correct designation and meaning of what
we do. It is true that in the Roman Church and in some
Protestant churches also there are those who speak of an
"altar." In our tradition and conviction we do not find an
altar in the New Testament. Neither our Lord nor his
apostles gave any suggestion of an altar. An altar speaks of
sacrifice and the New Testament speaks only of the sacrifice
of Christ on the cross. This was the "finished work of Christ"
and not to be repeated. "Christ was *once offered* to bear the
sins of many" (Heb. 9:28).

When we speak of the Communion we are using one of
the richest words of the New Testament. It is the Greek word
koinonia. This is translated, "to have a *share in*,' as in Romans
15:27, *"partakers"* of their spiritual things," or " to *give* a
share *to, go* shares with," as in Romans 12:13 — *"distributing*
to the necessities of the saints." This tells of the share one has

in the fellowship with Christ, a common experience of Christians, and this in turn is a shared experience with others of like mind. We receive and we give. We take and we pass on. We accept and we distribute. We are partners with Christ and then we are partners with other Christians.

1. *Fellowship with Christ*

This is the first mark of communion. We are in touch with the living Christ. This is *a personal* meeting. As the Christian is one with Christ, even as he is incorporated into the Vine (cf. John 15), so here we know we are one. The common meal of the East was used as the occasion of this fellowship. It was at the table where Jesus met his disciples. In the Upper Room at Jerusalem; in the home at Emmaus where he tarried; and later the disciples "continued...in the fellowship, and in breaking of bread" (Acts 2:42). When the Lord had gone, they could not take part with him in the supper meal of the day, but now in the special meal of communion they could share in fellowship with him.

The idea of fellowship speaks of oneness with each other. Jesus and his followers are sharers in the same life. This was a fellowship of faith, for only those who shared in that faith could understand and know. When people of another culture and language get together to speak or to sing, it is obvious that a light and glow comes to their faces in their fellowship of understanding with each other. The onlooker who does not know their language is shut out for a while and on his face is no radiance! How true this is at the Table where friend meets *the Friend of sinners.* Jesus there gives himself to his own and there is response. This fellowship is based on believing. They also suffered together. This is the *koinonia,* the partnership with Christ.

2. *Sharing with Other Christians*

The second mark of communion lies here. We are also in touch with others of like mind. This is *a social* meeting. At the Table we are with Christ as individuals, but we are also there with others in a common bond of faith and love. We are a community. At Pentecost it was said that "they were all with one accord in one place" (Acts 2:1). This is the fellowship of the communion "of the Spirit." Christians live in the company of the Holy Spirit and thus live in each others company. There is a sharing, one with the other. We do not live for ourselves. We are ready to aid one another. This is seen in our gifts of money and goods, and in practical ways of help. In the work and service of the church we are alongside each other. Friendship has a new meaning when we relate one to another "in Christ." True, we have loved ones and friends around us, but when we engage in this rite of love at the Table we are close to others of like mind.

A congregation as we are suggests that we have been "gathered together" by the drawing power of the Holy Spirit. We have been attracted to Christ as filings are to a magnet. We are now bonded together as God has brought us from various backgrounds. We now share in the same spiritual life and own the same Master. We are also "blood-brothers" through the blood of his cross. Thus in charity with each other we seek to put ourselves in the place of others in their need; to see and feel as God gives grace and understanding. We give and we forgive at the Table, knowing that we stand in the need of forgiveness.

3. *United with the Whole Church*

The church is not only here, but in the unseen. Multitudes have become part of the church victorious, while the rest of us is part of the church on pilgrimage. At the Table we have communion with Christ and through him we are linked to all his people in all the ages and throughout the world. This is *a universal* meeting. Transcending all race, color, creed, is the one great fact of our time that we have communion, fellowship divine, with all of God's people in the world now. Some may not yet allow us to sit down with them, but we do invite all of God's children to sit down with us. Not to do this is to deny the oneness of the Body of Christ. Failure to invite is to come short of our meaning of communion. We do not seek a union because we already believe in the unity of the church. This is a fact. We are "one body" and therefore act as such.

Because of this fact we also know that at the Table we are joined with the saints who have entered into their rest. We do not see them and we cannot go to them. With Christ present at the Table we believe that he brings with him the whole church in heaven and on earth. The unseen is greater than the seen. Where Christ is — there is the church. In this larger unity we rejoice for those who have left us in winning the victory over death and sin, and gladly give the hand of fellowship to all other Christians. Here we have found each other. "We, being many, are one body in Christ, and every one members one of another" (Rom. 12:5). Thus the communion is actual.

Our communion with the whole church indicates how universal this is. Imagine the whole church! Is this the church we know? Are we circumscribed by denomination or group? Are we limited to our own community? The church is now world-wide and this is the one major fact of our time. Even then we must also include the people of God in all the ages before us. We join hands with fellow-believers everywhere. We can never limit the church by our calculation or arithmetic. Where Christ is, there is the church. As he is present in the Communion service and at the Table of commemoration, we have fellowship with all of God's people.

VII. A Thanksgiving

My God, I am thine;
With a comfort divine,
What a blessing to know that my Jesus
*   is mine!*
In the heavenly Lamb
Thrice happy I am,
And my heart it doth dance at the sound
*   of his name.*

— Charles Wesley

VII. A Thanksgiving

"He took the cup and gave thanks."
— Matthew 26:27

Not the least important of this service is the spirit of praise and thanksgiving. We express our joy and gladness for his gifts in Christ. At the Hebrew Passover certain Psalms were sung called the Hallel. The title is taken from the repeated use at the beginning of some of the psalms of the word "hallelujah" — Praise ye the Lord. Psalms 113-118 provide the basis of this outburst of thanksgiving. Here are the "hallelujahs" sung by a grateful people. Our Lord shared in this at the time of the Passover and as he instituted the Last Supper which followed. During the meal there were occasions of thanks to God in prayer as our Lord "blessed" God and "gave thanks."

Thanksgiving is the expression of joy. This comes from a spirit released from sin. A heart of gratitude brings thanksgiving and praise. Instead of grumbling and complaining we are grateful. At the Lord's Supper in the Upper Room the spirit of disruption and division present among the disciples was changed to one of thanks as they carried out the Passover and the Lord's Supper and "sang the hymn" (cf. Matt. 26:30). Chiefly in prayer do we find this expressed in the actions of our Lord as he took, broke, and gave to his disciples. The solemnity of the occasion was permeated with the joy of thanksgiving to God.

1. *This Is a Eucharist*

The word has been used by some to denote a Mass or a sacrifice, but nowhere in the New Testament is it so used. The word used by our Lord *eucharisto* means simply "to give thanks." Thanksgiving is the expression of joy God-ward, and is therefore the fruit of the Spirit (Gal. 5:22). Believers are encouraged to abound in it (Col. 2:7). This is one aspect of the Lord's Supper often overlooked. In the solemn rite and ceremony which we rightly attach to the occasion we overlook the joy and gladness which springs up in thanksgiving. The injunction to prepare and examine oneself has clouded this other aspect which we have neglected. Even our hymns express little of this note in the stress upon the sacrifice and sufferings of our Lord.

Perhaps thanksgiving seems out of place at the Table? Surely we can be reverent and yet exuberant? When emotion wells up in pathos or tears, nevertheless there is still room for the thankful heart. Gratitude is a must when we recall our Lord's sacrifice and our salvation through him. We read that "Jesus, who for the *joy* before him endured the cross, despising the shame..." (Heb. 12:2). When our Lord fed the crowd (John 6:11) he "gave thanks." When he raised Lazarus from the dead (John 11:41) he "gave thanks." And now in the Lord's Supper, he "gave thanks." These three occasions teach us that this was no light or formal thing. This was the exuberant upsurge of gratitude to God for what he was about to do.

2. *This is an Ecstasy*

The mood of the soul when inspired by some high moment of worship is lifted up and there is an exultation of spirit. This is often expressed in deep emotion; an outburst of speech; or in singing. The "hallelujah" of the Hebrew becomes the praises of the Christian. At the Table we gather for a meal and a fellowship. The spirit is not entirely solemn and need not be sad. There is room for gladness and praise. This is a Supper and an occasion of joy. Gratitude for God's goodness has a place. No dirge on the minor key need be sung. No lament or complaint is here. We have found Him whom angels and all nature acclaim as the Lord of Glory. He has entered our life to redeem and save. Surely the note of exultation is suited!

Many testify to the uplift that comes from this service. Ordinary days and occasions are seen in the light of the special. This is a high and holy day for the Christian. We say our "Grace" and give our prayers of thanks for daily bread and all life, but here we exult in spirit more than usual when we recall to mind the cost of our redemption and the sacrifice of our Lord. When two women were tied to the stake on the seashore at Wigton, Scotland, in 1685, because they were Covenanters, the older woman was first drowned by soldiers to intimidate the younger woman. She was Margaret Wilson and she would not deny her Lord. Thus she sang the 25th Psalm — "Unto Thee O Lord, do I lift up my soul. . . ." In suffering and death she was able to exult in spirit and give thanks to her Lord. Jesus in his last hours also sang. We now look back in recollection and also sing.

3. *This Is a Eulogy*

A testimony of praise is here given by those who love the Saviour. Nothing can stop the soul from bursting out in glad expressions of thanks. Take the hymns we sing and read over the words once more. See how fitting they are as they bring us into the place of suffering and death. Meditate upon the thought of the writers and find yourself brought into a mood of solemn joy — solemn because of the sufferings of Christ, but joyful because of his victory over sin and death. Thus we enter into the meaning of the cross and into a new understanding of the Lord's Supper. Go back to the Passover and read in the Hallel Psalms (113-118) and recall some of the words of Psalm 116: "What shall I render unto the Lord for all his benefits toward me? I will take the cup of salvation, and call upon the name of the Lord. I will pay my vows unto the Lord now in the presence of all his people" (vv. 12-14). And then in verse 17 — "I will offer to thee the sacrifice of THANKSGIVING, and will call upon the name of the Lord."

The eulogy or blessing is not something done *over* the elements. *We do not "bless" bread and wine.* This is blessing and praising *God* in prayer and thanksgiving. The Last Supper meal anticipates the Messianic Banquet to come when Christ completes his victorious work. In this light we see the reason for the thanksgiving or eucharist. An African Chief visited Buckingham Palace by invitation to see Queen Victoria. He was asked — what did he think of it? He said, "I was most of all surprised to see myself there." So we give thanks when we realize we are invited to sit down with Christ!

The *eucharist* or *thanksgiving* is the heart of our experience at the Lord's Table. We are the nobodies who have been accepted in the Belovèd One (Eph. 1:6). What manner of love the Father has bestowed upon us that we should be called the sons of God (I John 3:1). All this inclines the heart to thanksgiving. Our hymns take on new meaning as we repeat the words. The words of Scripture bring new meaning and light as we enter into this heartwarming experience. "Thanks be to God for his unspeakable gift" (II Cor. 9:15).

Background:
  "When he had given thanks, he gave to them."
                                              — Mark 14:23
  "He took the cup, and gave thanks." — Luke 23:17
  "He took bread, and gave thanks." — Luke 22:19
  "When he had given thanks, be brake, and said."
                                              — I Corinthians 11:24

VIII. A Passover

I bind my heart this tide
To the Galilean's side,
To the wounds of Calvary,
To the Christ who died for me.

I bind my soul this day
To the brother far away,
And the brother near at hand,
In this town, and in this land.

I bind my heart in thrall
To the God, the Lord of all,
To the God, the poor man's Friend,
And the Christ whom He did send.

I bind myself to peace,
To make strife and envy cease,
God, knit Thou sure the cord
Of my thralldom to my Lord!
                        — Lachlan Maclean Watt

VIII. A Passover

"Christ our passover is sacrificed for us."
— I Corinthians 5:7

At the heart of our Christian faith is the fact that we are debtors to the Hebrew background. The Old Testament finds fulfilment and completion in the New Testament. No better illustration of this is found than that of the Passover. From the days of the Exodus in Egypt, Israel kept this feast as central to their faith. The church, the new Israel of God, keeps the Christian Passover in the Lord's Supper.

This is one of the neglected parts of the Christian's interpretation of the Lord's Supper. We are in danger of overlooking the Hebrew background. Our Lord as a son of the congregation and as a loyal Israelite observed the feasts and ceremonies of the synagogue and the Temple. The Passover stands out in significance for his own observance, especially for the last time. This was the occasion when our Lord introduced the Christian Passover which now we celebrate.

1. The Ordinance of the Passover

Looking back to the historical event is helpful for us. There in Egypt the Hebrew people were in bondage and slavery. They were under the lash of the taskmaster and subject to the cruelties of the Pharaoh. They had no rights or privileges. Moses was commanded by God to bring them deliverance. The method was unusual and in the eyes of some, foolish. A lamb for an household was taken and after inspection to see that it was without blemish, was killed and readied for the meal. The blood of the lamb was sprinkled by the head of the house on the lintels and door-posts of the house. The meal of roast lamb had with it bread, wine, fruits, and herbs. All was partaken as an act of faith in the promise of God to bring deliverance. That night the messenger of God visited Egypt in death: death to the firstborn of Egypt, but not death to the firstborn of Israel. This was so because God said, "When I see the blood I will *pass over* you."

Here is the word used to denote Passover. Under the shelter and sign of the blood of the lamb there was salvation, or safety. Thus the Israelite was ready to eat in haste and move out to a new life. The unleavened bread spoke of the haste, and the shared meal of the family a token of faith's solidarity. The act of the head of the household spoke of faith on behalf of others, honored by God. God commanded that this ordinance be kept a feast forever, a perpetual re-membrance of that exodus deliverance from slavery.

2. *The Upper Room Passover*

Our Lord as a lad went up to Jerusalem at the time of Passover and there had his conversation with the doctors of religion in the Temple. During his lifetime he would share in many Passovers. Now he comes to the last occasion and he is the host. The preparation is made by buying a lamb and setting up the place of the Upper Room in the home of one of his disciples. The basin of water and the towel are there, but he must take them when his apostles are bickering and one readies himself to betray him. Reclining around the table the apostles and Jesus carry out the ritual. There are four cups, the cup of Remembrance, the cup of Redemption, the cup of Salvation, and the cup of the Coming Kingdom.

They eat the unleavened (*Matzoh*) bread and share in the dish of friendship.

During this feast our Lord introduced the new ordinance in what we call the Lord's Supper. After the departure of Judas he took one cup, possibly the cup of Salvation, (cf. the author's *The Pathway to the Cross,* chap. VI) and gave this with bread to his followers. Bread is now the symbol in place of the lamb. Jesus, knowing that he would soon die on the cross as the Lamb of God, gives this new symbol to accompany the wine for the remembrance of his sacrifice. Linked with this activity are the words our Lord spoke in loving intimacy. They are recorded for us in John 14-17 and these bring strength and nourishment to our souls.

3. *Christ our Passover*

Looking back we trace the history of that first Passover at the time of the Exodus for Israel. Then we witness the last Passover at the time of the cross for Jesus. Now we are gathered around a table to celebrate the Christian Passover for our day and need. In the Upper Room there was also the singing of the Hallel Psalms and we keep up that worthy tradition. Our hymns speak of our faith, since what we believe is sometimes best expressed in what we sing. But the most effective way is in what we *do*. Here at the table we do something. Faith is expressed in act, and love is something we do. What richer way than in the Lord's Supper as we partake together!

In this Passover then we are expressing certain truths. We are not re-enacting the sacrifice of the cross. We are not engaging in a Passion play. We are preaching or proclaiming Christ's death. Bread and wine are not body and blood in a material sense, but as representative symbols of *the event* of Christ's death. Thus we celebrate with thanksgiving Christ's sacrifice for our sins. As Israel at Passover was delivered from slavery, so now the Christian has been released from the bondage of sin through Christ our Passover. As freedom came to them and a promised land, so now the Christian enjoys the liberty of the Holy Spirit and has found the eternal rest of the new life in Christ.

Today we are privileged to be one of Christ's disciples to sit with him at the Table and there remember the cost of our redemption. Jesus alluded to his approaching death as a sacrifice of atoning efficacy. He likened himself to the Passover Lamb whose death brought deliverance. This victory over sin and death becomes ours by faith. That is why we must now keep the feast.

When Paul wrote to the Corinthians he was writing to more Gentiles than Jews who had become Christian. It was necessary to relate the Passover in its new context. In so doing Paul called upon them to "cleanse away the old leaven" (cf. I Cor. 5:1, 8). At Passover time the house was purified and old things were thrown away. This became a symbol of a deeper purification. As we partake of this feast we vow to live a pure life in the midst of a sinful society. Thus God will "pass over" us in blessing and not in judgment.

Background:

> "This is the ordinance of the passover." — Exodus 12:43
> "They made ready the passover." — Matthew 26:19
> "I shall eat the passover with my disciples." — Mark 14:14
> "I have desired to eat this passover with you before I suffer." — Luke 22:15
> "It was the preparation of the passover. . . ." — John 19:14

IX. A Feast

Come to the feast, for Christ invites,
  And promises to feed;
'Tis here his closest love unites
  The members to their Head.

'Tis here he nourishes his own
  With living bread from heaven,
Or makes himself to mourners known,
  And shows their sins forgiven.

Still in his instituted ways
  He bids us ask the power,
The pardoning or the hallowing grace,
  And wait the appointed hour.

His presence makes the feast;
  And now our spirits feel
The glory not to be expected
  The joy unspeakable.

— Charles Wesley

IX. A Feast

"Let us keep the feast." — I Corinthians 5:8

In one sense the Lord's Supper was a farewell meal. Jesus had gathered for the last time with his followers. Here was said the "good-byes" of his earthly life. He told them that he must leave them (cf. John 14:1-6) and they were astonished and frightened at the thought of being left alone. Thus there has gathered around this observance the solemnity due to it. This has been further deepened by the knowledge of the sacrifice of the cross, so that we always come together with due reverence and dignity appropriate to the occasion. But just here we must not overlook what is a complementary truth that there is also the joyful note of the feast. The Passover in its deliverance brought a festal note into the occasion.

The Last Supper was a farewell meal, but at the same time an anticipation of the Messianic banquet. Not until the fulfilment in the Kingdom of God would Jesus again eat the Passover and drink the fruit of the vine (Luke 22:16, 18; Mark 14:25). A feast speaks of festivity and merriment, like a wedding feast has its accompanying fun and frolic. The guests make merry and are glad. How can we do this at the Lord's Table? Linger a moment to ponder this truth that it is a feast and not a fast. We are God's guests. The prodigal has returned home and there is now a feast provided (Luke 15:22-32). At the Table we are the prodigals who have come home to our Father's house and we are glad.

1. *A Family of Love*

If we think of our gathering as a family occasion we are more apt to catch the spirit of that Upper Room event. When Jesus met with his apostles he had no home of his own and was dependent upon his many friends for shelter and refreshment. The home at Bethany was one and the unknown disciple in Jerusalem in whose Upper Room they now met was another. Jesus was brought up in a particular family in Nazareth, but in his public ministry he gathered a new family — a family of the redeemed. We are part of that now.

The idea of the family suggests the place, the time, the relationship of a group bound together by ties of love. In such company it is natural to gather around a table and there talk, sing, and share with each other the deepest things of life and of faith. Table fellowship has something in it we do not find anywhere else. The Upper Room and the home at Emmaus remind us of this truth. In the simplicity of what is natural there is the profound experience of "belonging" one to another. We are a family of God. In other days in Scotland the Lord's Supper was celebrated at a long table, spread with white linen. An Elder stood at the end to receive the Token from those who came forward to partake. Those who came often came as families. First would be the father, then the mother; after them the sons and daughters. Today, the pew is covered with a white cloth, symbolizing that we all gather around a table and we do so as the household of faith.

2. *A Feast of Joy*

Associated with the Lord's Supper has been the idea of the love-feast. Here Jesus washed the feet of his apostles. Ever since, devout souls have copied this in enacting similar washing as preparation for the receiving of the bread and the wine. We may not all agree that this is the way to interpret our Lord's command and example (cf. John 13:14) but one thing is a "must" — we should enjoy this hour and let love burst out in joy and gladness. The smile of peace and the look of love should exemplify the deepest faith of our hearts. Are we not glad that God in Christ has loved us and saved us? As guests of God we are at a banquet. Eastern meals are noted for their lavish courses of food and drink. Time is spent without haste to enjoy eating and drinking. The humblest home and meal is graced by the leisure and love thus expressed.

This is a feast of life and not of death. Death is passed and accomplished now for us. We have entered into Christ's victory and triumph. The cross is empty and the tomb is empty! We are on the other side of the sacrifice and suffering. The light has overcome the darkness. Love has conquered hate. Instead of the spirit of heaviness there is now the garment of praise. A social occasion is always diffused with joy, and this is no exception. This is a feast and not a fast. Jesus was criticized in his ministry because he and his disciples did not fast when expected to do so. He was the Bridegroom and as at a wedding there would be seven days of feasting, so he enjoined joy and not sadness as long as he was there. At His Table we rejoice in his love and mercy.

3. *A Festival of Hope*

In looking back we have faith in the efficacy of Jesus' blood and righteousness. In looking up at the Lord's Supper we show love to our Saviour and to his own. And now in looking on we anticipate with hope the glorious future. We are carried into the eternity which speaks of a day of paradise. Jesus said, "I shall not drink again of the fruit of the vine until that day when I drink it new in the kingdom of God" (Mark 14:24, 25). When the Bridegroom comes for his bride, the church, then will be the final festival. The feast now is a foretaste of that festival of banquet and of song. Peter spoke of "the sufferings of Christ, and the glory to follow" (I Peter 1:11). This supper tells us of that coming day.

Thus it is that in this celebration there is gladness and not gloom; song and not lament; hope and not despair; splendor and not sadness. There is "the marriage supper of the Lamb" (Rev. 19:9). When all life can be sacred, we trace the use of the earthly symbols with heavenly and eternal meaning. At the Table we keep holy day and festival. This is the banquet of the King. We are at his Table. Mephibosheth sat at David's table and ate the king's meat (II Sam. 9:7, 8, 13). We sit at the table of a greater than David. We anticipate the crowning day and a share then in what he has promised.

Paul was eager to keep this feast (Acts 18:21). He observed the Church Year of that day and we may do the same. There is something gained by the periodic and regular observance of this feast which tells of our faith. When so observed Paul told his friends that it should be kept "Not with old leaven, neither with the leaven of malice and wickedness; but with the unleavened bread of sincerity and truth." If we are "sincere" we do not allow evil with good. If we have "truth" we do not allow the wrong with the right. Thus the feast is a time when we confess our sins and unworthiness and find forgiveness again to engage in the new life and the true life.

Background:

"Ye shall keep it a feast to the Lord for ever."
— Exodus 12:14
"I must by all means keep the feast." — Acts 18:21

X. A Legacy

Rock of Ages, cleft for me,
Let me hide myself in Thee;
Let the water and the blood,
From Thy wounded side which flowed,
Be of sin the double cure,
Cleanse me from its guilt and power.

Nothing in my hand I bring,
Simply to Thy cross I cling;
Naked, come to Thee for dress,
Helpless, look to Thee for grace;
Foul, I to the fountain fly;
Wash me, Saviour, or I die.

—Augustus M. Toplady

X. A Legacy

"I have received of the Lord that which also I delivered unto you." — I Corinthians 11:23

The last will or testament of anyone is a sacred trust. Our common life is familiar with the making of a will so that those who come after us are given their rightful inheritance of an estate. Whether a person has much or little this is stressed as a necessity in these days. Not always is the wish or intent of the donor or the one making a will carried out. As we reflect upon our Lord's last will and testament, we know that his bequest has been carried out to the letter. That is why we meet at the Table from time to time.

There is a sacred obligation in making a will. The last testament of any one is in a sense the last wish or word of that individual. It is also the final and fixed judgment of that one in bestowing his estate. This has far reaching repercussions. Sometimes a will is very simple and clear and direct. At other times a will can be complicated because of the various clauses and conditions set forth for special bequests. Our Lord's last wish was simple and direct.

1. *The Will Expressed*

The mind and thought of Jesus is here clearly unfolded in what he said and what he did. At the Last Supper our

Lord spoke in some detail concerning his last wishes. He used the Passover feast as the occasion to introduce the Lord's Supper (as we know it). In this fellowship meal the directives were given concerning its observance. The institution is carried out and the record tells of how Jesus "gave." In that one word lies the truth at the heart of this ordinance and sacrament.

To share in this feast it was necessary to be a true follower of him. Judas left the room before the New Covenant came into being. In discovering that will of Jesus it is clear that only those who love and serve him from the heart should be the ones to benefit from his last will and testament. It is true he imparted to them his peace and that is linked through the Table discourse (John 14-17) to the action in the Supper. Here he asks to be remembered perpetually. No direction is given as to how often, but the suggestion is there that it should be regular and continuous.

2. *The Bequest Received*

Not only did the apostles present receive this but the apostle Paul later writes to confirm it. Evidently the early church carried out our Lord's wishes. In their homes and in other ways and places they sought to remember him in this manner. Thus the tradition was firmly established in the local groups of Christians or churches when Paul was converted. He then continued this practice and in his *Letter to Corinth* refers to this event. In telling of having "received of the Lord" he also refers to the fact "that which also I delivered unto you." In these words he testifies not only to having received earlier the tradition then in use but also that he had passed on to others the will of Christ. He had this authority and as in the nature of the gospel (Gal. 1:14-17), so in the Lord's Supper, Paul received this directly from the Lord in revelation. Thus what was handed down (tradition) Paul knew, and with the added revelation from the Lord he was now able to give this to others.

The nature of this bequest may be seen in that two things

are involved. One is the "peace" given by Jesus (John 14:27) and the other is the "love" to be known (John 13:34). Peace is love resting and this his disciples possessed by the Holy Spirit. He called them his friends and told them to share the new life with others. This meant that love must act, even as he gave example in washing their feet. This beatitude of blessing rested upon those who did what he commanded. The final thing is the "example" to be shown by the disciples. This is part of the bequest. In loving deeds and kindly words the disciple acts accordingly.

3. *The Inheritance Shared*

Paul desired to give to others what he had received. In this the will of our Lord was carried out. The benefits and blessings are obvious in the life of discipleship. At the Table we share once again. There is a perpetual giving on our Lord's part. As inheritors of that estate we dare not keep it to ourselves. In receiving this we receive the gospel. In receiving the gospel we give it to others. The gospel is a received gospel. The ministry is a received ministry. The communion is a received communion. Everything we possess we have received of the Lord.

During Covenanting days in Scotland a young woman was challenged by the soldiers seeking out the Covenanters to arrest them. Did she know where they might be in that district? Where was she going? Her answer was simple — "I go to my Father's House to hear the Will read of His Son who has died." In that sentence lies the profound truth of what we have as inheritance. God's Son has died for our sakes. He has left his last will and testament. It is read in the New Testament and we hear afresh the wonderful words of life. We are included in the will and there is a bequest for us. We may take it now and then having received it, share it with others. This is the meaning of what we do and say now.

The heritage of the Christian is rich and abiding. Nothing can destroy it and no one can steal it from us. It is safe and secure in the eternal keeping of God. Take out your New Testament and read anew the glowing words of promise and fulfilment — and thank Him for remembering us in his will.

The last will of our Lord had in it the nature of a commandment. A command is not lightly overlooked. Many Christians act and speak as if the words of Christ were optional and not binding. Even as Jesus gave to his disciples in that last Supper, so he gives to all of his own a rich heritage. As Paul spoke of it, he had "received of the Lord," and that meant an acceptance of a gift. Paul did not conjecture what he might say to the church about the gracious teaching of .our Lord. He "received" it — by revelation in the power of the Holy Spirit. This is a binding experience of something never to be forgotten and therefore something to be shared by others. Thus Paul "delivered" this to the Christian church. He could not change or revise it in anyway. Paul had a "received" ministry. In the mold which gives its shape to what is cast in it, thus Paul gave it to us. Here is the final and incontrovertible act concerning the Lord's Supper.

In God's gracious design we have become the recipients of his bounty and grace. The "good will" announced in the Christmas gospel has been transmitted through the legacy "in Christ" and now confirmed in the last will and testament found in the Lord's Supper.

Background:

"He gave to the disciples." — Matthew 26:26, 27

"He gave to them." — Mark 14:22, 23

"He brake . . . and gave to them." — Luke 22:19

"When he had dipped the sop, he gave." — John 13:26

"A new commandment I give unto you." — John 13:34

XI. A Committal

Where have you been, my brother,
  For I missed you from the street? —
I have been away, for a night and a day,
  On the Lord God's Judgment Seat.

And what did you find, my brother,
  When your judging there was done? —
Weeds in my garden, dust in my doors,
  And my roses dead in the sun.

And the lesson I brought back with me,
  Like silence from above,
That upon God's throne there is room alone
  For the Lord, whose heart is love.

— Lauchlan Maclean Watt

XI. A Committal

"Let a man examine himself."
— I Corinthians 11:28

No one comes to the Table except in that spirit of humility. A sense of unworthiness steals over the communicant. We realize that what we do here is an act of deepest committal to Jesus Christ our Lord and Saviour. Aware of his presence we are profoundly moved in heart and devotion. All our worship at other times is now at the summit. Here we touch and taste things unseen. Jesus is closer than ever in our experience. Reverence is begotten within us and awe fills our minds.

1. *The Imperative*

"Let a man examine himself. . . ." Such a command is not treated lightly. In other days some of God's people took it so seriously that they often refrained from coming to the Table. This was true of many Highland saints in Scotland. They had developed a sense of unworthiness and they shrank from the hallowed act of receiving the elements from the Table. Self-examination is an opportunity to meditate upon the realities of our Christian Faith; to think of our Saviour and what he has done for us; but specially to pray that God would unveil to us any spirit or act not in line with what we are about to do.

Whatever the methods of the service or the place of meeting, there is a solemn sense of the fitness of things. Here the soul is called upon to engage in the profoundest act of worship. This examination may well have taken place in some hour prior to the actual service of communion. Before our modern days of rush and speed it was not uncommon for churches to hold a preparatory service, usually on a week night. Then the thoughts of all were directed to the solemn responsibility involved in the Lord's Supper. Then motives were searched and in prayer and sermon the worshipper got ready for the Sunday engagement. If one is to "prove" or "test" himself, this is something to be done privately and beforehand.

The student is tested by the examination; the soldier by the battle; the athlete by the race or event in which he participates — so the Christian is tested as he comes to the Lord's Table. What is my life before God? How have I been living? What are my motives and aspirations in life? Do I seek to glorify God? Have I wandered away and need to return?

2. *The Insights*

"So let him eat of that bread and drink of that cup." What are the implications of this experience? Here are two reasons for this:

(1) *There is a judgment upon carelessness.* We should not come in a casual or careless manner. If we share in the communion and lack discernment, then he that eats and drinks, eats and drinks judgment unto himself if he discern not the body. . . . But if we discerned ourselves we should not be judged. This is the crux of our sharing in this feast. The mind of the Christian may go through the motions of the ritual, but unless we have spiritual insight to see and know what we are doing, we have missed the significance of the rite. This is a means of grace, so we say. The common bread and wine are material items, but as used by faith and in prayer and devotion we are discerning through them the

symbols of Christ's broken body and poured-out blood. This is no longer an ordinary meal. It is the Lord's Supper of the communion in his body and blood.

(2) *There is a blessing upon spiritual discernment.* One of the rewards of sharing in this occasion lies in the opening of the eyes of our understanding to see what actually takes place. Onlookers can see the material actions. The spiritual mind sees the unseen through the seen, the eternal through the temporal. Paul reminds his friends that some of them have been "sick and weak, and some have died" because they shared in this feast in "an unworthy manner." The reprobate mind is that which carries out the ritual but has no reality. The outward motions are not matched by inward motives. A conventional act is no substitute for a consecrated attitude. Instead of judgment there can be blessing. Instead of physical and moral judgment in body and mind, there can be spiritual and moral power to live worthily. Is Paul suggesting that there is a relation between our moral and spiritual state of soul to our physical well-being and health of body? The whole man is in view, not some cut-off "soul" as over against a "body." Christ's man is one in psychosomatic life and all our acts affect the total life of our persons.

To know oneself then is important and imperative according to the ancients. To know oneself in the light of God at the Table is a deeper examination. Here is a committal to God with far-reaching results. Here we see ourselves as we are. Past actions, failures, pride, greed, lust — whatever has been hidden to the world is now unmasked before him with whom we have to do. In his holy light we see the stain and blight of sin. We seek forgiveness and pardon. We take peace and joy and power. We return unto the Lord. We renew our vows. We commit ourselves in this hour of self-revealing.

3. *The Implications*

Two people commit themselves in marriage with vows and a ring exchanged as a symbol and token of their love for each other. In the Lord's Supper we engage ourselves and pledge ourselves to our Lord and Master. A serviceman commits himself to this country in an hour of need and thus gives away his life to the government to do as it pleases with him. This may include hardship, sacrifice, or even death itself. But the committal has been made and cannot be withdrawn. Thus at the Lord's Table the Christian engages to live and spend his life for Jesus Christ our Lord and Master. This is no light or careless act. This is done thoughtfully and carefully We carefully weigh the consequences of that moment. With reverence we say that we are not our own, we have been bought with a price (I Cor. 6:20). We dare not come to that Table lightly lest we bring judgment upon our lives. We desire to see with discernment the inner meaning of our actions.

As Paul has enjoined "we are to eat or drink...to the glory of God" (I Cor. 10:31), so here at the Table in eating and drinking the Supper we glorify God. In the Roman world, part of the religious life of the heathen was the offering of sacrifices to the gods. As a means of opposing evil spirits people would offer food to a god. In contrast the Christian offers himself as a spiritual sacrifice (Rom. 12:1), but at the Lord's Table we take bread and wine — eating and drinking — all for the glory of God, the God and Father of our Lord Jesus Christ. In this committal we bring dignity, honor, and worship to the glory of God.

Background:

"So let him eat...and drink.... For he that eats and drinks unworthily, eats and drinks judgment to himself, not discerning the Lord's body." — I Corinthians 11:28

XII. A Satisfaction

I am not skilled to understand
What God hath willed, what God hath planned;
I only know, at His right hand
Stands One Who is my Saviour.

And was there then no other way
For God to take? — I cannot say.
I only bless Him day by day
Who saved me through my Saviour.

— Dora Greenwell

XII. A Satisfaction

*"Except ye eat the flesh of the Son of man,
and drink his blood, ye have no life in you."*
— I John 6:53

There was a time in youth when some of us watched and looked on at the actions of our parents and adults. We might share with them in the regular hour of worship, but sometimes we were not expected to take part in the Lord's Supper. Some children and young people are ready when others are not and faith can be real to them. However, in the wonder and mystery of it all, many questions arose. What was taking place? Why did they do that? Now we have some of the answers as Jesus and his disciples "made ready" for the Passover-Communion.

No doubt young children were puzzled by the actions of their elders. Hearing the words spoken in this connection made it more puzzling at times. How could people eat another Person? Was this what was known as cannibalism? Of course, understanding comes by knowledge and experience. Actually, here is the simplicity of the Christian faith even though there is profundity. Satisfaction is here.

1. *Because of the Mystery*

"Except ye eat the flesh of the Son of man, and drink

his blood, ye have no life in you." These profound words search the mind and stab the conscience. These words of our Lord were spoken at the time of the feeding of the multitude. Those who opposed him murmured because he claimed to be the Bread of Life from God. God the Creator feeds the race continually by bread, but only once did he send his Son to be the Bread of Life. Manna was given in the wilderness for physical need, yet Israelites died. The Bread of Life is given so that spiritual nourishment is given with eternal life.

Thus there is another truth. By his coming into our lives "The Word became flesh" and in his humanity we are offered "bread," for "the bread which I will give is my flesh for the life of the world." The Jews stumbled at this in some idea of cannibalism, although they must have known this was figurative. To eat his flesh and to drink his blood seemed impossible to the Jew who knew that the blood of animals might not be taken as food: "Be sure thou shalt not eat the blood; for the blood is the life; and thou shalt not eat the life with the flesh" (Deut. 12:23; Lev. 17:14, 15). But it is just here that Jesus offered himself and the mystery becomes clear in that we take him in the fulness of his life given in death.

2. *Because of the Meaning*

"Whoso eats my flesh, and drinks my blood hath eternal life; and I will raise him up at the last day." Abundant satisfaction is here in the knowledge that in this act of faith the Christian is nourished through the new life received. Christ's offer to sinful man is that of eternal life. This is the substance of Christian living. It is a new experience, yet valid in this life. It is God's gift and we do not merit it nor can we work to purchase it. Grace alone provides and offers this. Too often we think of what we are trying to do at the Table, when the all important truth is to dwell upon what *God* is doing. This is the action of God. We are only agents in what we do, for God is acting through us as well. Through the service he mediates and transmits himself to us in spirit and in truth.

We may not be able to define this mystery, but in experience there is the awareness of a power not ourselves. Its meaning brings satisfaction to the believing heart. Here in bread and wine we partake of Christ. Because he died, we died to sin. Because he lives in resurrection power, we live in him. Because he has given us eternal life, we shall share in resurrection glory. Goethe once said, "The highest cannot be spoken; it can only be acted." In that sense we speak of the Lord and act in the Lord's Supper. We never exhaust the meaning as new light breaks forth from time to time. We never cease to marvel at God's grace which permits us to share in this feast. Of one thing we are sure — that through Christ we have eternal life never to end and we renew this with him at the Table.

3. *Because of the Mysticism*

"He that eats my flesh, and drinks my blood, dwells in me, and I in him." Mysticism is not mistiness. The mystic is like a seer of old in that he sees steadily and whole. His eyes have been opened and his spiritual knowledge is real. He has passed from death to life. The old things have passed away. Everything has become new. At the Table the Christian mystic recalls the sacrifice of his Lord and in using the common elements set apart he enters into the deeper experience of oneness with God. Not by his own meditation or thought (as some have claimed), but in and through the use of the elements and the action with the Word of God. By this means he is caught up to hear things and see things in imagination beyond the dull routine of life. Now he is aware that he is *united* with Christ and is "far ben" with his Lord and Master. He is in the inner circle of his friends. He is also aware that he is *identified* with Christ in death and resurrection.

The symbols will disappear but the experience abides. Nothing bring satisfaction to the soul like this event. At the

Table there is a foretaste of glory to come even as we look back to the cross which opened the Kingdom of heaven to all who believe. The completeness and finality of Christian faith is achieved.

Nothing is more profound than simplicity. Everyone understands the meaning of "bread and water," yet, who can fathom the meaning of our Lord's words! The Jews then took them literally (v. 52 — "how can this man give us his flesh to eat?"), and so do others today in their priestly claims and ritual. The value here is wholly spiritual. Many have left the simplicity of Christ and have elaborated theological sciences and intricate creeds. We have worked out difficult symbolism and have given the impression that Christianity is composed of the impossible and inexplicable. Yet Jesus spoke simply of "bread and wine." As the manna in the wilderness was typical, so Christ is the reality of that which is symbol. Say to him now,

> Thou bruised and broken Bread,
> My life-long wants supply;
> As living souls are fed,
> Oh, feed me, or I die.

In living we seek fulness of expression and abundant satisfaction. What we see and touch and know through the senses passes away. The things seen are temporal, but the things unseen are eternal. That is why we find what we seek in Christ. In the Supper there is satisfaction through identification with him.

Background:

> "Whoso eats my flesh, and drinks my blood hath eternal life; and I will raise him up at the last day.... For my flesh is meat indeed, and my blood is drink indeed. He that eats my flesh, and drinks my blood, dwells in me, and I in him." — John 6:54-56

XIII. A Presence

10-5-97

They, with a stranger, broke the bread:
  "Do this; remember me!"
And all at once they saw — not dead —
  His true reality:
The outstretched hands, the love shed wide
  Of him that had, yet had not died —
And all the Life that was to be.

— Laurence Houseman

XIII. A Presence

> *"He was known of them in breaking of bread."* — Luke 24:35

The presence of a loved one is the token and seal of a constant love. Our human relations know this and we cling to it as necessary for our well-being. Even so it is with the spiritual relationship with God in Christ. The practice of the presence of God is most important to us who follow him. Personal relationship is a spiritual reality even though the person who is the object of our love is absent physically. There is an intuition of the soul which brings the loved one near. We do not feel we are alone. At the Table Christ is present in a real sense even though it is a presence-in-absence.

This is part of the reality of Christian experience. We testify to the presence of God with us. Brother Lawrence wrote his letters with the title *The Practice of the Presence of God,* now a spiritual classic. In that little book is the testimony of a servant man who worked mostly in the kitchen and told of his joy in being in the divine presence at all times. This is a truism of faith, but at the Lord's Table there is a sense in which we become aware of that presence to a greater degree.

1. *As We Commune and Reason*

The walk to Emmaus was the occasion for this experience for two disciples (Luke 24:14, 15). "Commune" has in it the idea of "talking together." Two people share with each other the deep things of God. In this conversation the most intimate relationship is established. Because of a common bond with their Lord these two find oneness and unity of heart. They are welded together. Their fellowship came not because they had anything in common from their past lives, but solely because they had each found Christ as their Saviour and Lord. This is where we find our unity today. John Bunyan tells of his conversion coming — in part — through hearing two women sitting at their door talking about the things of God.

They were also "reasoning" together and this means they were "discussing." They were weighing up what it meant to be followers of Christ. They were recalling the teaching and the events of his life. All the memories of the past were crowding in. They knew about his suffering and death and thought that this was the end of that wondrous ministry. In talking of all the things which had happened they conversed about their hopes and aspirations. Evidently they were disappointed that Jesus had not delivered their nation, and they were sad at heart in that he had died but had not risen from the dead. It was then that Jesus drew near and went with them (v. 15). His presence was there although they had not identified him at the first. They were in his presence although not aware of it. When we think of the Passion of our Lord; read about it in Scriptures; ponder over the story and talk with each other about it, he is near.

2. *As We Have Communion*

When Jesus met with these friends at table in the home at Emmaus he had been constrained to tarry with them. He made as though he would go further, but consented to stay with them. The custom of ending the ordinary meal with a simple act of remembrance concerning him and his

death had already developed. These two disciples — outside
the regular circle of the apostles — evidently had adopted this
practice. The meal here was not our Communion service but
a simple supper at the end of the day for refreshment and
hospitality to their guest. It was during that meal that they
became aware of the identity of Jesus. Was there something
characteristic in the way he broke the bread which reminded
them of what others had passed on about the Upper Room?

Jesus' friends knew about his ways. Now at the common
supper they began to add this simple rite which came to
be our Lord's Supper of the communion. They believed he
was still invisibly present when they enacted this. Today
we have come to set apart this event in a special ritual and
service, taking longer time and setting it apart from our
ordinary meals at home or at the church. Part of our belief
and faith is that the presence of Jesus is with us in a special
manner at the Table. Not that we think of this presence as
on the table, but *at* it. At the first he was there visibly and
personally. Now he is present-in-absence. Some Christians
have differed in describing this reality. The Church of Rome
teaches that the substance of bread and wine is changed into
the substance of the body and blood of Christ. This is an
attempt to give objectivity to the divine presence. Protestants
generally think of that presence as real and to faith actual
as we obey his command and use those elements as signs
and seals of his love to us.

3. As We Journey

Those two disciples walked a dusty roadway in despair
and hopelessness. Then Jesus came and in his presence life
and the future were transformed. God's presence in Christ
is for the highway as well as the holy place. Space is part
of God's creation and there is no place or experience of life
outside his orbit of contact or control. The veil of the unseen
is drawn aside when he comes to us. This he does at the
Table and on the road. From the communion we go back
to the toil and sweat of our daily bread. He is also with us

then. Sir Ernest Shackelton tells in his diary how he and two friends marched across an ice-cap in the Antarctic to seek help. When the journey ended, one of the three said, "I had a curious feeling all the time, that there was another Person with us." Shackelton lifted his head and answered, "So had I." "Lo, I am with you alway, even unto the end." "My presence shall go with thee."

The journey of life is an untraversed way for most of us. We have come part of the way, but the future is still unknown to us. On the way there are "resting places" or abodes where we must stop for the night. The oases in the desert were the places for travelers on foot or on camel. Here at the Table we have stopped or paused for a little on the journey and find refreshment. God is near. Christ is real. The Holy Spirit is present. We find our hearts and minds responsive to the divine pressure. While Jesus draws near in many ways, this experience at the Table is rich with meaning and lasting in impression. In our meditation about our Lord, and as we think and brood over the mystery of gracious love, we sense his presence. God comes down his secret stair and we hear that still small voice.

On life's dusty way we find differing experiences of life. There is the hour of suffering and sorrow — but he is near then. There is the hour of joy and gladness — and he shares that with us. In shadow or sunshine his presence is never withdrawn for he walks our highways and byways still.

Background:

"While they communed and reasoned, Jesus himself drew near. They constrained him, saying, Abide with us. . . . And he went in to tarry with them. . . . As he sat at meat with them, he took bread, and blessed and brake, and gave to them. . . . And their eyes were opened, and they knew him. . . . — Luke 24:15, 29-31

"Lo, I am with you always." — Matthew 28:20

XIV. A Chorus

Dear dying Lamb, Thy precious Blood
  Shall never lose its power,
Till all the ransom'd Church of God
  Be saved to sin no more.

E'er since by faith I saw the stream
  Thy flowing wounds supply,
Redeeming love has been my theme,
  And shall be till I die.
                              — William Cowper

XIV. A Chorus

*"When they had sung an hymn, they went
out into the mount of Olives."*

— Mark 14:26

One of the joyful aspects of the Lord's Supper is the singing of the people who share in it. True, the hymns are usually stressing the suffering and passion of our Lord. They point back to the cross with its sacrifice. They are sung with a reverence and solemnity fitting to the occasion. Nevertheless, to sing in a minor key is not to supress joy and thanksgiving. Without exuberance there is a deep and pervading feeling that here we are face to face with our Lord who loved us and gave himself for us. The moments are precious and sacred. Prayer and speech are hushed and only in song do we find the best means of expressing our faith in the finished work of our Redeemer.

At the Lord's Table we may find it profitable to take the hymn book or psalter and quietly read the words before we sing them. This is a means of heart-preparation open to all of us. Perhaps memorizing some of these majestic hymns is also a means of grace worth emulating. Across the centuries Christians have found their oneness in the hymns they have sung. The early plain song has given way to more intricate tunes, and these mixed with certain songs of the gospel lift up the heart in readiness for the Lord's Supper. We find a chorus of song everywhere.

1. *In the Upper Room*

At the celebration of the Passover there was the singing of the Hallel Psalms — 113-118. These were usually antiphonal: one member of the table fellowship recited the text and the others responded to each half-verse with "Hallelujah." Our Lord must have shared in this singing. None of the Gospel writers has reported about this, and only reverent imagination can recall that he was the Host for that occasion and leader of the ritual. These Psalms should be read as a preparation for the Lord's Supper as they provide the background for our praises.

The one characteristic emphasis of the Hallel Psalms is that of *Thanksgiving*. Each Psalm has the spirit of prayer as the psalmist and the devout Jew offered up his worship to God and praised Him for deliverance. They trusted in the living God and were not put to shame. "O give thanks unto the Lord; for he is good; because his mercy endureth for ever" (Ps. 118:1). Jubilation and praise burst forth around that table in the Upper Room. Then it was that at the closing hymn or psalm "they went out to the Mount of Olives." Following praise came betrayal. After the Supper came the seducer. After the sacred came the profane. Jesus went to the Garden of Gethsemane and his arrest with the strains of the Hallel Psalms in his mind and heart.

2. *In the Church*

During our hours of worship we use the psalms and hymns with spiritual songs to our profit and uplift. A service of worship — with communion of the Lord's Supper or without — is not complete unless we can express our praises to God. As a vehicle of worship it has become one of the finest avenues of expression. All the moods of the soul are there through the poetry and the music.

The early church took over the *psalms* of the Hebrews

as the first Christians were Jewish in background. Thus the chanting and singing was easily a part of Christian worship. Then according to the writers of the New Testament other poetry was written and became the *hymns* of the church. We have extracts of these in various passages (cf. Phil. 2:5-11; I Tim. 3:16) . Finally, the church was led to compose *spiritual songs* using the gifts of the people musically so that over the ages these have had full and varied use. At the first it is obvious, however, that "teaching and admonishing one another with psalms, hymns, and spiritual songs, with grace singing in your hearts to God" simply gives the idea of three words for the one act of praise. The use of musical instruments also was not overlooked from ancient times.

We can take the hymnbook and meditate in the words of the matchless hymns — "O sacred head now wounded," "When I survey the wondrous cross," "Jesus Lover of my soul," "Twas on the night when doomed to die," "The Lord's my Shepherd," "Here, O my Lord, I see thee face to face," "Bread of the world in mercy broken," "Jesus, the very thought of Thee." Whatever favorite hymn we prefer, our spirits are touched and prepared for the reception of the Lord's Supper.

3. *In the Glory*

The book of the Revelation anticipates a banquet and a gathering of singing people. "They sung a new song saying, Thou art worthy" (Rev. 5:9) ; and, "They sing the song of the Lamb" (Rev. 15:3) . Other hints are given of the multitudes who throng around the throne and *sing*. Music is the language of heaven. All redeemed souls can enter into this choir. Here is the grand chorus. All parts and levels of song are here. There is harmony after the discords of time. The music has a lilt in it not produced in our earthly experience. The new song celebrates the victory of Christ over sin and death. The kingdom has come in finality and fulness. Christ as the sufferer and conquerer is central in the praise. These hints find clamax in the Hallelujah Chorus (Rev. 19:6, 7) when the whole world acclaims him as Sovereign Lord and King.

It is this which we anticipate at the Lord's Table. We look back in thanksgiving to the cross, but we look on to the crowning day. Here we make melody in our heart because we look for the day of victory. When our Lord left the Upper Room he went out to tragedy — with a song on his lips. Every trial of life for us can be faced — with a song in our heart. The genius of the Christian faith lies here — in its capacity to sing in the darkest hour. *Sursum Corda* — lift up your hearts! We lift them up to the Lord!

One thing is certain in the church. We will never cease to sing God's praise. Whenever spiritual renewal or revival has come to the church there has been a corresponding outburst in song. This was true in Old Testament times, when the temple was built under Solomon (cf. II Chron. 5:11-14). Then the people and the singers sang their praises to the sound of music. In the days of the Evangelical Revival in England, Charles Wesley set the people to sing even as brother John proclaimed the gospel in preaching. Wesley, Isaac Watts, and John Newton — to mention a few — are the forerunners of many others giving the church its hymns to sing. Here at the Table we may well sing with exaltation. Moving with solemnity at the first as we think of Christ's betrayal; and celebrating the rite with due respect for its sacrificial cost; we pass finally to the joyful notes of God's goodness and grace enduring for ever, as in the Twenty-Third Psalm.

Background:

"Singing in psalms, and hymns, and spiritual songs."
— Ephesians 5:19; Colossians 3:16
"They sung a new song, saying, Thou are worthy."
— Revelation 5:9
"They sing the song of the Lamb." — Revelation 15:3

XV. A Renewal

Let us break bread together,
On our knees, on our knees.

Let us drink wine together,
On our knees, on our knees.

Let us praise God together,
On our knees, on our knees.

When I fall on my knees,
With my face to the rising sun,
O Lord, have mercy on me.
— Negro Spiritual

XV. A Renewal

"If ye know these things, happy are ye if ye do them." — John 13:17

In the preparation for the Passover and the Lord's Supper, Jesus had an unnamed disciple provide the house and the Upper Room and two of his apostles to secure the lamb and see that everything was as planned. "There make ready" (Mark 14:15), he said. One other thing needed to be done, and that our Lord did during the feast. His followers had gathered but they disputed who should be the greatest (Luke 22:24) and no one had done the work of the servant or slave in washing the feet of all who had come (John 13:10). Here our Lord stepped in and did this. His beatitude, or blessing, in the text suggests that when knowledge is a part of the heart, then blessed or happy are we in obedience.

We must beware because disloyalty is treachery and Satan may be at the supper! It was so then, and could be now. When Christians scramble for position and place, and wrangle about honors in the shadow of the cross, what is possible even now? Do we not need renewal of spiritual life, especially in the realm of our motives? Why are we here and what is our intention at the Lord's Table?

1. *As a Servant — in Love*

The setting of the Upper Room never knew anything like

this on other occasions. Here was enacted a drama which would move the heart and compel the will. The catharsis of the emotions was drastic in its impact upon these twelve men who had gathered to meet with the Lord. He had planned this feast and he was their host: they were his guests. Little did they think of the unusual experience they were to face that night.

Jesus knowing that his hour had come to face the cross, having loved his own in the world, he loved them to *the end* (v. 1). This is not solely to the end of their lives or of his. The word has in it a deeper meaning in that it speaks of the goal and yet of the fulness and completeness of that which is done. He loved them completely, not partially; eternally, not changeably. This was love in its fulness and thus Jesus washed their feet. He acted quietly and deliberately so that they were rebuked for their selfish thoughts and actions. They were disputing who should be the greatest in the kingdom of God, and then Jesus came to manifest his love in this particular way. He was their Master and here he was serving them as a slave-servant would. None of them had the right spirit to serve him in his last hours: he served them. Thus he loved them to the uttermost with a love which would see them through the ordeal and fiery trial to follow.

2. *As a Disciple — in Lowliness*

The lesson was an acted one, a demonstration in deeds, not in words. Jesus who knew God as one with God, yet stooped to take the towel and the basin in this drama of humility. The greatness of God is seen not in his throne of glory but when he stoops to wash men's sin-stained feet. Jesus was not arrayed in princely robes but in the rough garment of the worker. Adding the towel gave him a symbol of washing and cleansing never to be misunderstood thereafter. Peter was to remember that act, for later in life he wrote: "Be clothed with humility" (I Peter 5:5). He recalled the knotted towel around the Master's waist.

If there would be anything a disciple would do it would

be to please his Lord and Master. To translate the teaching into action would be the supreme end of hearing and obeying what the Lord had said. And yet here it is in reverse! Discipleship implies discipline — the self-control of the body and of the mind. The twelve apostles were unmasked in their worldly and secular spirit far removed from the spirit of Jesus. Their inward, hot, and jealous notions of one another are seen to be shameful, sinful signs of their true nature. Outwardly they were at the Table to be ministered unto; inwardly they were far away and unworthy for this. Yet, our Lord knelt before each one in turn and washed his feet. What did Peter think in his disturbed mood of indecision? What did Judas think when he looked down at the Lord at *his* feet?

3. *As a Friend — in Loyalty*

The spirit of the Lord is that of love and lowliness. The thoughts of the Twelve Apostles were those of hate and pride. Only what Jesus did cast out the demons which beset these men. In his action of washing their feet he forever challenged their pettiness and littleness. The way of greatness in the Kingdom was the way he demonstrated and which was a preview of the coming cross where the Suffering Servant of God would lay down his life for them. These men failed their Lord in that crucial hour, but they would each recover (although not Judas).

Let us remember that loyalty is the sign of true love. This quality of life and devotion never alters and nothing can separate those who are bound together in this fashion. In the Passover the Hebrews were no longer slaves waiting on their taskmasters: they had become princes and princesses before God. Now in this Passover-Lord's Supper of the Upper Room Jesus told his own that they were no longer slaves but his friends. As friends they would share his secrets and be partners in the kingdom of God. In washing their feet he had used the ordinary, everyday way of hospitality to bring to them the cleansing of their conscience and life.

His example is not to be forgotten. We, today, are bidden to follow his steps. We are to wash one another's feet. The truth from him is to cleanse us and we in turn share with others. Here is the basis of spiritual *renewal*. If we know, blessed are we if we do. Obedience is the divine way of spiritual blessing. Knowledge is entwined with doing. The truth is obeyed. At the Table we enter anew into the meaning of this renewal, and meeting with our Saviour we are renewed in the inner man.

The omission of any reference to the actual institution of the Lord's Supper by John has puzzled some. The answer is likely that John wrote long after this memorial was established and celebrated throughout the Roman Empire. Also, the other Gospels and Paul's writings had been circulated among the churches. Here he reports only what was said at the time of the rite and assumes the rest is known. There is a knowledge which brings information but does not call for action. Such is history looking back. But in this case our Lord is reminding the disciple that *spiritual knowledge* calls for *obedience and action*. This is the way of renewal. this is the beginning of remaking a life and character. There is a knowledge of the head, but this is the knowledge of love and of trust. Such knowledge is the means of renewing the Christian life into fulness.

Background:

"There was also a strife among them, which of them should be accounted the greatest. . . . And Jesus said unto them . . . I am among you as he that serveth. . . . And I appoint unto you a kingdom. . . . *That ye may eat and drink at my table in my kingdom.*" — Luke 22:24-30

XVI. A Triumph

Lord, I am weary, lonely, full of fear.
Hush, my beloved, my strong love is near.

Father, I falter, failing in my place.
Hush, my beloved, Christ will give thee grace.

Father, To-morrow daunts me, gard and gray.
Mine is To-morrow. Conquer thou To-day.
— Lauchlan Maclean Watt

XVI. A Triumph

*"The Lord Jesus the same night in which
he was betrayed took bread."*
— I Corinthians 11:23

Jesus did many things that night. It was a night to be
remembered. Everything in his public ministry came to
its climax then. This was also the prelude to the cross and
its death. That was the dark night of the soul — of Judas.
It could have been a dark night for our Saviour, but he
turned captivity captive and overcame the powers of evil.
This is what takes place not only in the Upper Room but
when we gather at the Table of Communion. We come from
the world without and are beset by the flesh and the devil.
Each contends for the mastery, the price of which is betrayal
of our Master. Here we trace how our Lord won his victory
and so may we.

The night is the time of darkness. Then comes evil to
disturb and beset us. The deeds of darkness are evil. The
night time becomes the occasion of much that is wrong. That
is why we think of the night as a symbol of deeds of darkness
and evil. The Christian is urged to put off the deeds of
darkness and to put on the armor of light. When Jesus came
to that last night with his apostles he engaged in a spiritual
conflict. Only enemies attack but a friend betrays. Our Lord

knew the tragic sense of life when this took place. Yet it was in that hour of hours — the same night — when he won his greatest victory.

1. *Blessing Overcame Betrayal*

Judas had plotted and schemed to end the public life of Jesus by his bargain with the Jewish authorities. They had convenanted together to betray Jesus. Judas was the agent to be used because of his closeness to the Master. Imagine this man spending three years in such close relationship, hearing his teaching, watching his gracious works, and then stooping to betray his Master! When the woman came with the alabaster box of very precious ointment and poured it on the head of Jesus, Judas, you recall, was the one who objected by his criticism. Then he showed how his mind worked: it worked in terms of money, by setting a price on everything. There are some things which cannot be so priced!

Over against the devotion of that woman is the denial of Judas who now dwells in darkness and not in the light. The woman came to serve the Lord but Judas knew only servility and not love. The most beautiful act of life is to lavish love upon Jesus. The basest is to deceive him. Yet in spite of this act of Judas, our Lord took bread that night and instituted the Supper which we still commemorate. That is victory and not defeat. In the midst of betrayal our Lord poured out his blessing upon those men who trusted him.

2. *Goodness Overcame Greed*

A startling contrast is here. On the one hand, the greed of Judas. On the other hand, the goodness of Jesus. Judas pretends to act in a good way toward Jesus. He continues as one of the apostolic band, even when his heart has gone from Jesus. He attended the feast when he knew what he would do. The forces of evil had so gripped him that he was swept on, unable to stop. Jesus appealed to him; made the gesture of feet-washing, then giving him the dish of friendship. In that last act Jesus did all he could to save Judas.

Judas played a part, put on the mask as the hypocrite or actor, and pretended to be a friend of Jesus. No more damning sin is found than that which betrays love. The kiss later in the garden was the seal of evil for Judas.

Thirty pieces of silver was the price of a slave and for this Judas sold his Master. Judas played his part by pretence. Outwardly to the other apostles he was still the treasurer of the band and still a friend of Jesus. In that dark night in the garden the dark night of the soul lay bare. His kisses (for this is in the plural — "he kissed him much") were a mockery. He pretended to be good but his was counterfeit goodness. If an enemy attacks us openly with hatred or jealousy we know how to face this, but when an enemy comes with a smile and a kiss we can be deceived. This kiss of Judas wounded the Lord far more deeply than did the nails which fastened him to the cross.

Yet in spite of this act of Judas, our Lord took bread that night and instituted the Supper which we still commemorate. That is victory and not defeat. In the midst of avarice, covetousness, and greed our Lord manifested the goodness of his heart in trusting those men who obeyed his word.

3. *Devotion Overcame Denial*

The devilry which moved Judas to his act of betrayal and his own doom is in sharp contrast to the devotion of our Lord to his own men. In one sense all are traitors! At least the seeds are there within the heart. Judas was such for money and what it stood for. Others might sell the Master for reasons not connected with money! Peter denied his Lord for shame he might be linked with the Lord as a follower. Pilate tried neutrality because of fear lest he lose advancement in high places. The lie we speak or act, the non-involvement we claim in the struggle, the sparing of ourselves from sacrifice, and much more — we might say, "Is it I, Lord?"

Jesus believed in his men and in spite of their frailties and possible defection (like Judas) he kept on loving and trusting them. When the story was told it might have read: "the same night in which he prayed that High Priestly prayer," or "the same night in which he washed their feet," or "the same night in which he kept the Passover." Instead, we have this report "in the same night in which he was betrayed...." It was *then* — in the darkest hour, the cruelest moment, when Judas sat next to him in a place of honor waiting to stab him in the back — that our Lord instituted the Lord's Supper! Instead of evil, there is grace; instead of treachery, there is love. When you and I come to the Table, we can be assured that whatever *our* sin has been, there is forgiveness and renewal. Devotion overcomes denial. Grace is greater than all our sin.

Thus we trace the victory of grace. Grace is the word which is splashed across the pages of the New Testament to let all know how God treats sinful men. Grace is the outgoing heart of God to the undeserving. Recall if you will that scene in the Upper Room. There is Judas who will betray his Master, yet our Lord washes his feet and then passes to him the dish of friendship in the Passover feast! All that love can do is done. The shadow of that betrayal was even then over the soul of Jesus, yet he continues to carry out his duties as the host for that occasion. Knowing the foul deed planned, and seeing the soul of Judas as the salve of evil, Jesus did not falter. The washing of the apostles' feet after the supper was about over, and the comfortable words to be spoken, it was thus our Lord acted and taught. It was in that *hour,* in that *night,* he instituted the Lord's Supper and thus signalized his victory. Before the end of his talk to them he would say, "Be of good cheer; I have overcome the world" (John 16:33).

Background:

"The hour is at hand, and the Son of man is betrayed into the hands of sinners." — Matthew 26:45

"Father, the hour is come; glorify thy Son, that thy Son also may glorify thee." — John 17:1

XVII. A Tryst

For the bread, which Thou hast broken;
For the wine, which Thou has poured;
For the words, which Thou hast spoken;
Now we give Thee thanks, O Lord.

By this pledge that Thou dost love us,
By Thy gift of peace restored,
By Thy call to heaven above us,
Hallow all our lives, O Lord.

With our sainted ones in glory
Seated at our Father's board,
May the Church that waiteth for Thee
Keep love's tie unbroken, Lord.

In Thy service, Lord, defend us,
In our hearts keep watch and ward,
In the world where Thou dost send us
Let Thy Kingdom come, O Lord.

— Louis F. Benson

XVII. A Tryst

"There make ready for us."
— Mark 14:15

The language of the Lord's Supper is the language of love. In all the literature which speaks of the intimacy of soul with soul and life with life, nothing surpasses this story. The world has known many outstanding trysts of man with woman. The Brownings and the Kingsleys are noted for their devotion in married life. David and Jonathan are remembered for their lasting friendship, as are others. Here our Lord gives himself to his followers in a love never failing and in a self-giving unsurpassed even unto death. We may well speak of this as the trysting hour when we meet the One we love and there is the interchange of words and acts which manifests the heart-felt confidence in each other.

To be ready for a solemn hour of remembrance; to prepare for a religious occasion; to anticipate the most important decision of life — this becomes an hour when a decision is made and the soul meets God. Our Lord left nothing undone when he undertook the pathway to the cross. On that sorrowful way he manifested his love to his own as he met with them for the last time.

1. The Physical Preparation

The apostles were told by our Lord that the Passover would

be eaten at a certain house in Jerusalem. Evidently they did not know the place or the name of the disciple whose home was to be readied for that occasion. Two of the apostles (Mark 14:13) were sent into the city. They were to look for a man bearing a pitcher of water. This was unusual as the women usually did this service. They were to follow this man to the house. There the large upper room was for their use. As in most Jewish homes of any size that room would be entered by a stairway up to the roof so that privacy was secured. The lamb had to be bought adjoining the Temple, inspected, and then killed for roasting. The dish of friendship, the bitter herbs, the bread and a few other items were also procured. The room itself was furnished by the owner of the house and we would assume that he or the man-servant attended to the actual meal and the setting of the low table with its couches around.

Our preparation demands that we come with alertness. Do we get sufficient sleep the night before? Do we arise at a suitable hour so that we can carry through our morning needs at home before setting out to God's house? Do we arrive in good time so that we are in our seat before the service begins? Unless an accident or an unusual event has taken place, it is right and proper that we are here on time. Imagine a lover being late to meet his sweetheart! Christ is the Bridegroom and the church is his bride. The human relationship is based upon the divine. His disciples need to make the physical preparation in good taste.

2. *The Mental Preparation*

Many and varied are the ways for this. Before coming to church, either the night before or early that morning, a quiet time of prayer and meditation would be helpful. Before the service begins the hymnbook affords a means of grace. To read some of the hymns associated with the Lord's Supper or that of the cross prepares the mind to dwell upon that sacrifice. The Scriptures selected to be read in the service provide a basis for meditation. Listening to the strains of the organ or just being still and quiet and engaging in prayer are agencies of preparation also.

There is also the wider and larger preparation of the mind open to all. Our homes should have a bookcase of books among which will be some to help us in the Christian life. Money spent on these is an investment. There are the classic books of devotion coming to us from the past. *The Practice of the Presence of God,* by Brother Lawrence; *The Greatest Thing in the World,* by Henry Drummond; *The Pathway to Prayer,* by Samuel Chadwick; *The Diary of David Brainerd*; and the *Private Prayers,* by Lancelot Andrewes and countless others — these are available for the still hour when we drop everything else for moments of devotion in the presence of God. Reading the Bible and prayer is the foundation but these other choice books give us a special shelf peculiarly our own. Thus the mind is enriched for communion.

3. *The Spiritual Preparation*

Out of the mental background of thought and devotion we are prepared to set our hearts in deepest gratitude to God for all his benefits. As we meditate and reflect we are taken into the inner meaning of what we are about to do. In this service of communion we shall sing praises, and words take on a new meaning. Our words judge us and here we need to be careful as we sing that we express what we believe. In some services and churches the congregation is asked to recite *The Apostles' Creed*. This is the oldest and simplest of confessions of faith. The words join us with God's people across the ages of history and link us with all his people who confess him as Saviour and Lord now. In Scripture and in prayer we also prepare ourselves as we wait for the serving of the bread and the wine.

At last we take that bread and drink that wine. We ask God to be cleansed from sin and especially our sins of pride, jealousy, greed, and lust. We ask God to feed us with the Bread of Life and to nourish us with strength for whatever is before us. "Here, Oh, my Lord, I see Thee face to face...."

This is a trysting hour. We meet with the One we love. He is mine and I am his. The language of love is appropriate. The soul is hidden with Christ in God. We are in the body and yet we are with Christ. Time and space seem no more as we dwell for a moment in the eternal. We are caught up in faith and imagination to God's throne where Christ is seated at the right hand of God. All authority is his. We are his by his sacrifice and love. We are not our own. We belong to him.

It is not simply, "there make ready:" it is "there make ready *for us."* He, too, prepared himself and prepares us to receive. Did he not say, "It is more blessed to give than to receive?" He gives now and we receive from the pierced hands. Such is the thought and intention of this theme. The trust of the soul with God can take many forms. We may find God at the burning bush as did Moses; or see him display his power at Mount Carmel as did Elijah; or be overcome with his majesty in the Temple as did Isaiah. Trysts with God are made when a babe is born to a couple; or when marriage vows are exchanged; and when standing by a lonely grave. There are moments of splendor in the setting sun over the ocean and the splash of color in a variegated garden of flowers. The hour and the place are redolent with memories when we know we have met with God.

At the Table a special moment is our's with the one who loved us and gave himself for us. "Greater love hath no man than this. . . . Here is love, not that we loved God, but that he loved us, and gave himself for us. . . ." Whatever the word in heart and mind the experience is the same – we are wrapped up in the knowledge and love of God.

Background:

"Watch and pray, that ye enter not into temptation,"
— Matthew 26:41

"Watch ye, stand fast in the faith. . . ."
— I Corinthians 16:13

"Blessed is he that watcheth, and keepeth his garments,

lest he walk naked, and they see his shame."

— Revelation 16:15

"Let us not sleep, as others; but let us watch and be sober." — I Thessalonians 5:6

XVIII. A Mystery

And can it be that I should gain
*   An interest in the Saviour's blood?*
Died He for me, who caused His pain?
*   For me, who Him to death pursued?*
Amazing love! how can it be
*   That Thou, my God, shouldest die for me?*

No condemnation now I dread;
*   Jesus, and all in Him, is mine!*
Alive in Him, my living Head,
*   And clothed in righteousness divine,*
Bold I approach the eternal throne,
*   And claim the crown, through Christ, my own.*
*   — Charles Wesley*

4-10
98

XVIII. A Mystery

"I am the bread of life." — John 6:35

Any meditation on this theme must go to the source, the starting-point, by looking at the record found in the New Testament. There are five passages: three records of the Lord's Supper in the Gospels of Matthew, Mark, and Luke; and Paul's statements in I Corinthians 10 and 11. These are the source passages. There is, however, this passage in John's Gospel, Chapter 6, which necessitates consideration. In the instinct and faith of the church this is associated with the communion of the Lord's Supper. There is a mystery or secret here, just as Paul in dealing with the subject of marriage also speaks of a mystery (Eph. 5:32). Whatever our views may be in the interpretation of the Lord's Supper, there is always the feeling that when we partake we are in the presence of a mystery. Something is taking place which transcends all that we know. The believer is aware that he is in union with his Lord and Saviour.

John 6 is one of the profoundest chapters in the New Testament. Here we are in the presence of something transcending the ordinary mode of speech. The Jews of that day stumbled at the words of Jesus in their attempt to keep the text without the spirit. Thus they missed the deeper meaning of what our Lord said. "Eating" and "drinking" are not to be taken in a literal sense, but suggest the clearest way of individual, personal taking of Christ into our lives. This is what is known as "faith" in other contexts. There is nothing mysterious about this, even though it contains mystery.

1. *The Analogy of the Imagination*

Analogy is used in speech to convey profound truth. In this connection bodily functions become the means of explaining and interpreting our spiritual functions. These are not merely figures, but analogies, like birth, sustenance, digestion of food. Our education in this is based upon simple facts. Christian faith speaks of trusting Christ, but there has to be something which is like that of eating in the body. Thus we speak of receiving him into our lives until all that he is becomes part of us. Just like food, he strengthens our innermost being. What food is to the body, so Christ, the Bread of Life, is to the spirit.

Cultivating the imagination the Christian "sees" and "knows" spiritual truth as real. Christ came as a Teacher, Master, and Saviour. In the last of these aspects he died the death of the cross "for us men and our salvation." Thus if we receive him as Saviour we are also feeding upon him as that spiritual Bread which came down from heaven. Here we focus our thought upon the redemptive act and find hidden and secret strength. In memory of that death we take the bread and the wine in the communion. At that moment we are not eating and drinking the physical and material elements and nothing else — then we are also eating and drinking of Christ spiritually and mystically. Thus we feed upon Christ's death and passion. We identify ourselves with him in that death.

2. *The Unity of the Mind*

As we meditate at this feast of remembrance our minds are active. Our thought-life is alive in reading the sacred words of the institution of the Lord's Supper. We meditate upon these words and think them through. What do they mean? What do they suggest to us in our faith? What is the mystery which is hidden within the act? There is *a mystical union* with Christ. When Jesus spoke to the crowd (John 6) he was telling the outsiders of something which would be hidden from them. They would not be able to understand what he said. Only his own, the initiated ones, would understand and even then incompletely. This is the privilege of the elect, to those who are on the inside. The natural man cannot understand the things of the spirit. The language of John 6:35 indicates that Christ is the Bread of Life and he is more than manna. Manna kept people alive for a while but it did not give Life.

John 15, spoken in the Upper Room, carries this idea a step further. As sharers and receivers of divine gifts, the believer is also made a friend of Jesus. There is not only the mystical union with Christ — there is also the *identification* with him. What he went through we now pass through. We remember his death but we now affirm our death in him. As we are one with him so we identify ourselves with him in his sufferings and death. In the allegory of the vine and the branches we find a fitting story of our relation to Christ. His life flows in us and we are one with him in everything.

3. *The Community of the Heart*

Imaginative reason brings us to accept this truth that we are linked with all those who profess the same faith. "In Christ" is no mere shibboleth. It is spiritual reality. From the *union* and *identification* we come to *communion*. In this oneness and closeness of heart with heart we share the same life and obey the same will. In John 17 our Lord prays for his apostles, and also for all those who will believe on him in the ages to come. The whole church is thus in the heart of God. Because we are his, so are we one with all others. This may not express itself in a gigantic organization, but it certainly expresses itself at the Lord's Table. There every

Christian finds unity. We belong to a community, the fellowship of the twice-born.

This community transcends all other attempted unities. Politics unites some; education and culture unites some; social classes unite others; race or nationality unites others; but the one unity greater than all is that of the Lord's Table. In the hymns we sing; in the words we read; in the prayers we offer; in the message delivered; and in the actions we perform, we find the unity of the mind and heart. When Jesus spoke in John 6 of his approaching death he used figurative language to establish the spiritual essence of the Lord's Supper. The mystery is the secret of how God in Christ gives himself to us and we become one.

There have been those in the church who have taken this chapter and read into it, a sacramental interpretation. This is to make of the Lord's Supper a means of salvation whereby the sinner may find life eternal. Generally associated with the repeated acts of partaking of the "sacrament" this has come to be a substitute for conversion. The Reformers objected to this in their view of the grace of God alone bringing salvation. The "works" of man cannot save. We believe the sharing in the Supper is for the Christian believer. We should not, of course, rule out the possibility of God meeting a seeking soul at this hour should one come repentant and believing. Without faith the ritual cannot help. With faith the believing man finds Christ. Christ is the "food" of eternal life. We feed on Him by meditation on his words, and by communion with himself, of which the Lord's Supper is a perpetual reminder.

Background:

"I speak concerning Christ and the church...."

— Ephesians 5:32

XIX. A Friendship

But what to those who find? Ah, this
Nor tongue, nor pen can show,
The love of Jesus what it is,
None but His loved ones know.
— Bernard of Clairvaux

When I survey the wondrous cross
On which the Prince of glory died,
My richest gain I count but loss,
And pour contempt on all my pride.
— Isaac Watts

XIX. A Friendship

"Ye are my friends, if ye do whatsoever I command you." — John 15:14

Our Lord has been speaking at the Passover out of which he instituted the Lord's Supper. The Upper Room discourse reveals the intimacy and the closeness he had with his own followers. They were tied to him that night with ties of love and devotion. Judas we know marred that occasion. In that room and on that occasion there was a living union of the Lord and his disciples. Vine and branches are intertwined as one. Sap and fruit are interrelated in unity. Life abides and abounds as faith and obedience respond to the word of the Master. Love and loyalty are expressed one to another in the shadow of the cross. Joy and suffering are close together in the thought of victory over sin and death. Here was inaugurated the most significant partnership known to man.

We know that friendship given is not to be despised as a cheap thing. Some human friendships are given casually and carelessly. We read of people getting together through social contacts or economic ties and quickly entering into engagement and marriage. Such so-called friendships do not as a rule last very long. They lack the basis of true and lasting friendship. Our Lord's choice of his disciples was not done without forethought and a night of prayer. He knew what was in man and needed not that anyone should tell him what was in man. He also saw the potential in each of those whom he chose at the first.

1. *The Choice of Friendship*

This is the miracle of divine grace when we think of those chosen by Jesus. After a night of prayer he chose the twelve apostles to be with him and to follow him. A man is known by the company he keeps. This is a test of his friendships. Friendship affects character and the whole of life is influenced by those we take into our inner circle. The vicious and evil corrupt whereas the kind and loving enrich. Friendship implies a sharing together, an interchange of mind and heart. There is an intuition and feeling that we belong! The heart has reasons of its own, not known to the mind. There are degrees of intimacy, but true friendship knows no reservation of interest.

Friendship passes over differences of age, occupation, background, education, skills; and it is given and never merited. In that hour there is an equality of life with life not found anywhere else. Our Lord's friendship given to his own was part of the background of the Passover. There in that ancient feast the slaves in Egypt were given the time to sit for a meal although in haste. They were accustomed to stand and wait upon their masters. Now for once they could recline as princes and princesses of Israel. In that feast was the dish of friendship in which they dipped one with another as a sign and seal of their partnership in afflication. Now they would go forth to the promised land and afterwards recognize that the most enduring friendship was forged in suffering. Our Lord used this background and spoke to them as "my friends."

2. *The Fruits of Friendship*

Love issues in obedience to the Lord. Jesus asked his own to keep his commands. He implied that if they loved him that would be inevitable and possible. He had chosen them and set them apart to bear fruit. A new character was born and a new life was on the way in its development and potential. The practical values of life are spoken of as the most important in our busy, utilitarian age. But here our Lord stresses something greater — the partnership of the friend one to another. This is to be cultivated and not neglected. Men who have fought for their country in one of the services are usually those who later find a common kinship and vocabulary. Comradeship is one of the finest forces in life. The Musketeers of Dumas' novels lived by the oath: "Each for all, and all for each." Something of this spirit lies at the heart of Christian friendship.

Vines die unless pruned and cultivated. So with friendship and the partnership of Christ and his own. "No longer do I call you servants [slaves], for the slave knoweth not what his Lord doeth; but you I have called friends, because all things which I heard from my Father, I made known to you." The slave has his orders and his spirit is to obey, perhaps in fear. But the friend is one who shares the thought and mind of the Master. To cultivate friendship issues in fruit, the fruit of a godly character. Here is no time-server, but a lover who counts all else as nothing if only he can serve his Master.

3. *The Wreck of Friendship*

Great literature reports many instances of choice friendships: David and Jonathan; the Brownings; the friendship of Jesus in laying down his life for all. Even as friendship can be nurtured, so it can be eclipsed by disloyalty, treachery, and disobedience to love's highest and best. This is the tragedy of Judas. Three years in the Lord's company, hearing all the teaching, watching the miracles, and given the last moment to dip again in the dish with Jesus — all that and then he spurns friendship. Friendship is tested inevitably. Can it stand the strain of adversity or loss? What will change do to it? When friendship is disrupted the scars remain. Secrets once shared turn to acid. Only in agreement can two walk together. How tragic when the wear and tear of life disrupts and disagreements come.

Memory can aid us to rebuild fences and renew friendships once broken. Whatever our state of heart before the Lord's Table we are assured of forgiveness and pardon from our Master. He can renew and remake. He can restore the wasted years. As in the Upper Room he offers his friendship again. It is for us to receive. We may set limits to human friendships, but our Lord knows no boundaries to his friendships. His is the higher friendship and life is an education in love with him. That is why in the Lord's Supper we take anew this partnership and pledge once more our love and loyalty. He has already done this in his cross.

The cost of friendship is not to be overlooked. "Greater love hath no man than this that a man lay down his life for his friends . . . ye are my friends . . ." (John 15:13). When Jesus faced the last night with his own he saw the cup to be drunk in Gethsemane and he shrank back for a moment. Nevertheless, he went on beyond that to the cross — "for the joy that was set before him." Thus he endured the cross. That is why the Lord's Supper reminds us of the cost of friendship. Here is something transcending human friendship. Abraham was known as "the friend of God," yet how much more are we honored with that eternal friendship in Christ, never to be withdrawn!

Background:

"The church of God, which he hath purchased with his own blood." — Acts 20:28

"Him that cometh to me I will in no wise cast out."
— John 6:37

"Rejoice because your names are written in heaven."
— Luke 10:20

XX. A Service

Here we have seen Thy face,
And felt Thy presence here;
So may the savor of Thy grace,
In word and life appear.

The purchase of Thy blood,
By sin no longer led,
The path our dear Redeemer trod
May we rejoicing tread.

In self-forgetting love
Be our communion shown,
Until we join the Church above,
And know as we are known.

— Aaron R. Wolfe

XX. A Service

"After the same manner also."
— I Corinthians 11:25

Every time we come to the Lord's Supper we do so because of our Lord's command to remember him in this way. In so doing we establish a practice or habit from time to time. This repeated act in turn sets up a pattern of action or a ritual. We tend to repeat and do the actions in a familiar way. Whether we belong to a church with fixed ritual or prefer a church with a loosely connected way of worship the actions tend to become repetitious.

The word "liturgy" was used in the Roman Empire for public services rendered to the State. It was also a term used for service in the temple. The writers of the New Testament seized upon this familiar word for public worship and Luke reported that in the church at Antioch "as they ministered to the Lord" Paul and Barnabas were called and separated to special ministry (Acts 13:2). The "ministering" is the word used for *liturgy*. Whatever the particular use or work done, the New Testament always gives the meaning as *service to God*. Here at the Lord's Table is a service so rendered. "The same manner" and "for as often" suggest a special form of service.

129

1. *A Service of Worship*

The highest act of the Christian is to worship. In worship we give worth to God. There are many valuable things in life and we cherish them. There are individuals whom we love and honor above others and so give worth to them. But when we stand in the sanctuary we give God the supreme value and offer to him the obeisance due to him. In praise and prayer, in reading and sermon, we worship God. This is true when we offer our gifts and dedicate our lives. But this is also a fact at the Lord's Table. At the Table we express the worship of God in a unique way. Not only do we sing and pray, read and listen, but we use elements in actions which manifest the magnificence and beauty of God.

When Moses gave the command to keep the Passover these words were used: "Ye shall observe this thing for an ordinance to thee and thy sons forever. And it shall come to pass, when ye be come to the land which the Lord will give you ... that ye shall keep this service. And it shall come to pass, when your children shall say unto you, *What mean ye by this service?* That ye shall say, It is the Lord's passover. ... And the people bowed the head and worshipped" (Exod. 12:24-27). The close association of the Lord's Supper with the Passover suggests that in the new covenant we have a service of worship. No other act of worship brings such a sense of God's presence. Everything is heightened for a while. We are the guests of God and in these moments we carry out a liturgy or ritual of an ordinance God-given. In these unusual acts we bow and worship Him who has loved us and died for us.

2. *A Service of Devotion*

Allied with the act of worship is the fact of the love and loyalty we give to our Lord and Master. The command to remember Him in this way is an opportunity to manifest our devotion. Disloyalty to the highest was shown by Judas in the night of betrayal. Peter also faltered in his devotion but recovered. We may have failed and sinned but here we can renew our vows and show the fealty of our hearts. In the Halley Psalms of the Passover is Psalm 116 with verses 14 and 18 repeating, "I will pay my vows unto the Lord now in the presence of all his people." Paul said in Romans 10:9, "that if thou shalt confess with thy mouth the Lord Jesus, and shalt believe in thine heart that God hath raised him from the dead, thou shalt be saved." This is freely re-translated, "if thou shalt confess *Jesus as the Lord*" the evidence of salvation.

Devotion in this light is never in secret, but in public. The life must have the lip testimony supporting. The service of our country demands an oath of allegiance, a salute to the flag, a wearing of a uniform as evidence of that loyalty. Both psalmist and apostle unite in this — that a believer in the facts of the ritual must show to others publicly that he stands here. No traitor or craven spirit is to be tolerated. The Table of the Last Supper is the place where we stand at the salute! The communion is a service of devotion, an act of loyalty to our Master.

3. A Service of Grace

Everything in this service speaks of grace. The basis of God's dealing with the Israelites in the Passover deliverance was grace. God did not select them because of any goodness or merit. They were "nobodies" and yet God chose them in his mercy. Likewise, the Christian has not been selected because of anything in him to merit God's attention. We are sinners. Christ came to save sinners. By his mercy he has come to us. It is of grace and not of works, lest any man should boast. Boasting is excluded. All praise and glory belong to God alone. Such is the basis of our redemption. At the Table then we attest to this — that we are sinners saved by grace. "Naught have I gotten, but what I've received. . . ."

At the Lord's Table we proclaim anew the wonders of divine grace and mercy. We have been forgiven. We have been given faith. We have received fortitude to live as belonging to God. At the Table we testify that we stand in

grace. Now as we partake anew of the elements — the signs
and seals of God's mercy — we receive grace continually to
be humble and take from his outstretched hand. "Nothing
in my hands I bring, Simply to thy cross I cling" is the
fitting language of our heart. No man is worthy to receive —
yet it is in our unfitness that we have the means of receiving.
Thus the Lord's Supper is a means of carrying through a
ritual which proclaims the divine basis of grace and mercy to
sinful men.

There have been those in other days who shrank back
from sharing in the Lord's Supper. A sense of unworthiness
prevented them from partaking. A heightened awareness of
sin and guilt kept them away from the Lord's Table. Especially was this true where rigorious preparation was demanded
of the would-be communicant. In Scotland, as well as on the
Continent among the reformers, many shrinking souls were
debarred from the means of grace in their terrible feeling of
guilt and unworthiness.

On the other hand, we may come too easily and casually
to the Lord's Table. Where the rite is observed weekly it
is possible to miss the rich meaning in coming without much
or any preparation. Christians must decide which is prefer-
able. Certainly, some preparation is needed. Prayer, fasting,
meditation on the Word of God, the use of hymns and
psalms, and a period of quiet — these are ways of God's
preparation of the heart to receive the means of grace. Yet
grace in itself flows when we "remember Him" and we must
believe that as often as we do this "God comes down the
soul to greet, and glory crowns the mercy seat."

Background:

"For as often as ye eat . . . and drink."
— I Cornithians 11:26
"And thus shall ye eat. . . . Ye shall keep it a by an ordinance for ever. . . . And in the first day there shall be an
holy convocation. . . ." — Exodus 12:11-17

XXI. A Season

Here, O my Lord, I see Thee face to face;
Here would I touch and handle things unseen,
Here grasp with firmer hand the eternal grace,
And all my weariness upon Thee lean.

This is the hour of banquet and of song,
This is the heavenly table spread for me;
Here let me feast, and feasting, still prolong
The brief bright hour of fellowship with Thee.

Too soon we rise; the symbols disappear;
The feast, though not the love, is past and gone;
The bread and wine remove; but Thou art here,
Nearer than ever; still my Shield and Sun.

— Horatius Bonar

XXI. A Season

"When the hour was come, Jesus sat down."
— Luke 22:14

One of the choice expressions heard in other days concerning this experience was "the communion season." There are different seasons of the year in our calendar. There are "times" for everything in human life according to Ecclesiastes 3: "To every thing there is a season, and a time to every purpose under the heaven. . . ." Then follows a list of those "times" or "seasons" which fill out our time and destiny. There is "the time to be born, and a time to die; a time to weep and a time to laugh; a time to love and a time to hate. . . ." When the catalog is completed we notice something is missing. Ecclesiastes tells of man's aspirations towards God and in relation to human values of life. Everything is judged "under the sun" and by human standards. The New Testament has an extra to all this, although the end of Ecclesiastes suggests that to "fear God, and keep his commandments is the whole of man." That wholeness is not found until man finds God in Christ and out of worship he finds opportunity to manifest his love to God. The Communion "season" is one of those high and holy occasions.

1. *A Sacred Season*

In that Upper Room Jesus sat down at the appointed

hour. The preparations had been made by the apostles selected and the good man of the house. Everything was ready and furnished. There was no haste and there was no careless engaging in this most awesome event. Centuries of history had passed for the Jews and Jesus was an heir of that heritage. He was conscious of his racial connection and as a son of the congregation he shared in the festivals and ceremonies of his people.

All life is sacred in God's sight. His presence is everywhere. Yet there are times when all this is heightened for the believing soul. Such an hour is the communion season. There is a feeling of awe and reverence begotten within us. The circumstances converge to make it so — the solemnity associated with our Lord's betrayal and death; the elements received in memory of his dying love; and the surrounding hymns or psalms with the Scripture readings and prayers. All this tends to make the season sacred. Reverently we come to the Table of the *Lord*. As citizens come to a king or president; or when bride and bridegroom come to their wedding ceremony, so with the coming to the Lord's Table, there is a special sense of the solemnity of the occasion.

2. *A Joyful Season*

Jesus had set his face to go to Jerusalem. Now the end was near. The strain would soon be over in the sufferings and sacrifice of the cross. At the Passover-Table the preview of divine giving was portrayed. Then our Lord said, "With desire I have desired to eat this passover with you before I suffer: For I say unto you, I will not anymore eat thereof, until it be fulfilled in the kingdom of God" (vv. 15-16). The intensity of spirit is unveiled here as our Lord unbared his heart to his own. Next to these words of confidence in the final triumph of his kingdom came the words of warning about the betrayal (vv. 21-22). The sacred, holy experience of that hour was broken by the dark line of judgment soon to fall.

At the same time the season of remembrance was shot

through with joy and gladness. The coming kingdom was spoken of with assurance and confidence. The thanksgiving for all of God's gifts was offered in blessings and prayers to God. The psalms were sung from the Hallel with joy and hope. Jesus "for the joy that was set before him endured the cross..." (Heb. 12:2). In that light we see light. However grim was that dark night of the soul, nevertheless, our Lord exulted in spirit knowing the victory ahead. When we are at the Table we, too, share the same victory. The words and actions of that Upper Room have been carried down the centuries for the church to repeat. In so doing we are telling again "the old, old story of Jesus and his love." No other season compares to this. Christmas comes with the Bethlehem story and Easter breaks with its morning of glory, but every Communion season repeats the assurance of our acceptance with God in Christ. Thus the joy of the Lord is our strength.

3. *A Reserved Season*

The time for Jesus was providentially planned and enacted in that Upper Room. Jesus sat down with his apostles. They shared the feast together. Nothing could alter that fact. We, too, find similar experience to be true. This special season — whether weekly, monthly, quarterly, or annually — brings its own reward and enrichment. Many in other days in Scotland found it to be so when celebrated in the Highlands in the open air among the hills. The pastor would preach from a wooden pulpit and the people sat on benches or on the grass of the hillside, or under the shade of the trees of some glen. Then the table would be "fenced." This was a Scottish and Reformed custom to reserve the communion for those who were truly believers. How to find out was not easy. In the words and sermon solemn warning was given to the unconverted not to partake unless they repented. The Christian was reminded of his need of renewal and recovery from backsliding. The little lead token was received from those who had been visited by the elders as a sign of good standing.

Our Lord in the last hour of the Garden after the Upper Room spoke to those who hated him: "This is your hour, and the power of darkness" (v. 53). In the providence of God it ceased to be that because of the Lord's Supper and its prophecy. Reserved as a season of victory, we now find it the season of banquet and of song. If we have a reserved seat it is through God's grace. He is our Host and we are his guests.

The season for communion is always one to be remembered. The congregation with its gathering together; the spirit in the singing of familiar psalms and hymns; the ready listening to the words of the institution; and the passing of the bread and the wine. In some churches the people go forward to a communion rail, there to receive the elements one by one. This stresses *the personal nature* of the rite. In other churches the servants of God, the elders or other officers, go from the table to the pews — there to pass the plate and the cup to the waiting people. Every pew is part of the Table (and in Scotland a white cloth is placed over the pews as well as over the Table) and symbolically all are seated around this. This mode of serving stresses *the congregational or gathered community as one body* receiving the elements.

This is a solemn occasion. Jesus had an intense desire to celebrate the Passover. We do this because of him. He thought of us then. We think of him now.

Background:

"It is enough, the hour is come; behold, the Son of man is betrayed into the hands of sinners." — Mark 14:41

"This is your hour, and the power of darkness."

— Luke 22:53

Postscript . . . .

Three creedal statements or confessions of faith give help:

The Thirty-Nine Articles, article XXVIII., Episcopal Church

> "The Supper of the Lord is not only a sign of the love that Christians ought to have among themselves one to another, but rather it is a Sacrament of our Redemption by Christ's death: insomuch that to such as rightly, worthily, and with faith, receive the same, the Bread which we break is a partaking of the Body of Christ; likewise the Cup of Blessing is a partaking of the Blood of Christ.
>
> Transubstantiation, or the change of the substance of Bread and Wine in the Supper of the Lord, cannot be "proved by Holy Writ; but is repugnant to the plain words of Scripture, overthroweth the nature of a Sacrament, and hath given occasion to many superstitions. The Body of Christ is given, taken, and eaten, in the Supper, only after an heavenly and spiritual manner. And the means whereby the Body of Christ is received and eaten in the Supper is Faith.
>
> The Sacrament of the Lord's Supper was not by Christ's ordinance reserved, carried about, lifted up, or worshipped."

> 1571. Prepared for the Church of England

The Westminster Confession of Faith, chapter XXIX., Presbyterian Church

> "Our Lord Jesus instituted the sacrament of his body

and blood, called the Lord's Supper, to be observed in his Church unto the end of the world, for the perpetual remembrance of the sacrifice of himself in his death, the sealing all benefits thereof unto true believers, their spiritual nourishment and growth in him, their further engagement in and to all duties which they owe unto him; and to be a bond and pledge of their communion with him, and with each other, as members of his mystical body. In this sacrament Christ is not offered up to his Father, nor any real sacrifice made at all for remission of sins of the quick or dead, but a commemoration of that once offering up of himself, by himself, upon the cross, once for all, and a spiritual oblation of all possible praise unto God for the same: so that the so-called sacrifice of the Mass is most contradictory to Christ's own sacrifice, the only propitiation for all the sins of the elect. Worthy receivers, outwardly partaking of the visible elements in this sacrament, do then also inwardly by faith, really and indeed, yet not carnally and corporally, but spiritually, receive and feed upon Christ crucified, and all benefits of his death: the body and blood of Christ being then not corporally or carnally in, with, or under the bread and wine; yet, as really, but spiritually, present to the faith of believers in that ordinance as the elements themselves are to their outward senses."

1647. Prepared for the Presbyterian Church of Scotland

The Heidelberg Catechism Question 80. What difference is there between the Lord's Supper and the papal Mass? *Answer.* "The Lord's Supper testifies to us that we have complete forgiveness of all our sins through the one sacrifice of Jesus Christ which he himself has accomplished on the cross once for all; (and that through the Holy Spirit we are incorporated into Christ, who is now in heaven with his true body at the right hand of the Father, and is there to be worshipped). But the Mass teaches that the living and the dead do not have forgiveness of sins through the sufferings of Christ unless Christ is again offered for them daily by the priest (and that Christ is bodily under the form of bread and wine and is therefore to be worshipped in them). Therefore the Mass is fundamentally a complete denial of the once for all sacrifice and passion of Jesus Christ (and as such an idolatry to be condemned)."

1563. Prepared for the Reformed Church in Germany, the Netherlands, Hungary, and the United States.